River of Time

JON SWAIN

River
of Time

ST. MARTIN'S PRESS ☙ NEW YORK

A THOMAS DUNNE BOOK.
An imprint of St. Martin's Press.

RIVER OF TIME. Copyright © 1995 by Jon Swain. All rights
reserved. Printed in the United States of America. No part of
this book may be used or reproduced in any manner whatsoever
without written permission except in the case of brief
quotations embodied in critical articles or reviews. For
information, address St. Martin's Press, 175 Fifth Avenue,
New York, N.Y. 10010.

Library of Congress Cataloging-in-Publication Data

Swain, Jon.
    River of time / Jon Swain.
        p.   cm.
    ISBN 0-312-16989-2
    1. Indochina—Description and travel.   2. Swain,
Jon—Journeys—Indochina.   3. Cambodia—History—
Civil War, 1970–1975.   4. Vietnam—History—
1945–1975.   5. Indochina—History—1945–
I. Title.
DS535.S95   1997
959.604'2—dc21   97-19586
                                                               CIP

First published in Great Britain by William Heinemann Ltd

First U.S. Edition: October 1997

10   9   8   7   6   5   4   3   2   1

To the memory
of my Mother and Father

Two things greater than all things are
The first is Love, and the second War.
And since we know not how War may prove,
Heart of my heart, let us talk of Love!

Rudyard Kipling

Contents

Acknowledgements

River of Time would have been harder to achieve without the help of many people. I am indebted to François Bizot and his enchanting family. Bizot, who has kept faithful to the best French ideals in Indo-China, lent me his beautiful house on the Ping river in Chiang Mai to write. My thanks go, too, to Xandra Hardie, my agent, and Tom Weldon, my editor at Heinemann, for their encouragement and perseverance. Acknowledgement is due to the *Sunday Times* in which some passages first appeared. I particularly appreciate the help and support of Josceline Dimbleby, who kept the book on course. I am grateful to numerous journalist colleagues and friends but must mention Donald A. Davis, William Shawcross, Lucretia Stewart, Tiziano and Angela Terzani in Bangkok and Nici Dahrendorf, who encouraged me to get this book started. My greatest debt is to Claudia, my wife, and Pia, my daughter, for their love, tolerance and understanding.

I would like to say here a special word about Michael Davis O'Donnell. There were days when covering the war in Vietnam was brightened by one individual. Captain O'Donnell, a helicopter pilot assigned to the First Aviation Brigade based at Dak To and Pleiku in the Central Highlands of Vietnam, was one such man. He is dead now. His helicopter was shot down on 24 March 1970, attempting to rescue eight American soldiers. He was an amateur poet who left behind a legacy of poetry which his friends at Camp Holloway were sensitive enough to save and give me.

Reading the slim booklet of his poems *Letters from Pleiku* for the first time on a chill morning as I waited for a chopper ride turned my day around. I have kept it with me ever since to remind myself of the simple truths that one American fighting man said about the Vietnam war. Because his poems meant so much to me and to others in Vietnam at that time I have included some of them in this book.

Finally, I would like to conclude with a personal note. I owe a great debt to several journalists who made, in my view, the time in Cambodia and Vietnam the silver-age of war reporting. I would like to single out particularly Donald Wise, Gavin Young, Don McCullin and the late Neil Davis, film cameraman, killed in a tinpot coup in Bangkok on 9 September 1985.

There are no simple truths about war reporting. But in his apartment during the Vietnam war Neil hung a plaque. 'When you walk with me do not walk behind me for I may not always lead, do not walk in front of me for I may not always follow, walk beside me and be my friend.' For me, it says it all.

APV,
London,
June 1995

Chronology

1954

Defeat at Dien Bien Phu marks the end of France's Indo-China empire. Vietnam is divided by the Geneva Accords into communist North Vietnam, under Ho Chi Minh, and western-backed South Vietnam.

1965

United States pours in ground troops to defend South Vietnam, crumbling under a communist insurgency supported by North Vietnam.

1968

Communists launch Tet offensive in which they attack more than 100 towns and cities across South Vietnam. By now, there are more than 530,000 American troops in South Vietnam, American planes are bombing North Vietnam, and the Americans are engaged in a secret war in Laos against the communist Pathet Lao and the North Vietnamese army. Only Cambodia, under Prince Norodom Sihanouk, has avoided the bitter wars that have torn through Vietnam and Laos. For the US, Tet is the political turning point of the Vietnam war when the Americans realise they will never win and begin the process of withdrawal.

1970

In Cambodia, Sihanouk is deposed by his right-wing Defence Minister, General Lon Nol. Following the coup, the Vietnam war spills over into Cambodia. The US arms Lon Nol, while the Cambodian communists, the Khmer Rouge, are backed by communist North Vietnam and China, growing into a cruel, disciplined force.

1973

Paris Peace Accords are signed giving the US the diplomatic means of withdrawing the last American forces from South Vietnam and having its prisoners returned. The war goes on.

1975

Khmer Rouge tightens siege of Phnom Penh and on 12 April US marine helicopters evacuate US embassy and other foreigners from the beleaguered capital. Five days later Khmer Rouge forces capture Phnom Penh.

Deprived since the 1973 Peace Accords of US bombing and logistical support South Vietnamese forces also shed ground, and on 30 April they are defeated and communist troops finally capture Saigon.

1975–1979

Cambodia is convulsed by the Khmer Rouge revolution. Massive exodus of Boat People from the two halves of Vietnam, united under communist rule. Laos, too, becomes a communist state.

Lands of
the Living Past

By now, so many journalists have written their war stories about Vietnam, Cambodia and Laos that another book at this late stage may be thought superfluous. Their stale, wearied refrain is 'I remember when I was in Indo-China . . .'

If I am guilty of a similar sin and sound too much like an old Indo-China hand, I apologise. The exploitation of nostalgia is not my intention. If I romanticise some aspects of war, put it down to youthful exuberance. The countries of what was formerly French Indo-China are lands that still stand apart from the rest of Asia, though they no longer make such tragic headlines.

Even as they are being modernised by the West they remain aloof, tragic, beautiful and provocative, a bewitching medley of the senses. They are places which have coloured my experience of life like no others on earth. I regret that I ever had to leave them, though I recognise that I did not get to know them as well as I should and that I saw them at a moment of dark tragedy when they were cockpits of conflict, decaying under foreign armies, ideologies, internal oppression.

The impact of the wars upon Indo-China has been terrible, the communist victories a hideous disillusionment. But through these

3

lands flows one constant, the Mekong. Great rivers have a special magic. There is something about the Mekong which, even years later, makes me want to sit down beside it and watch my whole life go by.

The Mekong is the longest river in Southeast Asia. It begins its life tamely as a small glacial spring in the Tibetan Himalayas, the roof of the world. Then, fed by melting snow and mountain streams, it tumbles down through sheer-sided gorges in southwestern China, twists and turns through the jungly hills of Laos, descends through a series of rapids into Cambodia, then flows, at a more leisurely pace now, into southern Vietnam to meander peacefully into the South China Sea below Saigon.

Between 1970 and 1975, I lived in the lands of the Mekong – Cambodia and Vietnam – and forayed into Laos to report on America's secret war there. This book is primarily a personal account of those tumultuous days. During this period the Mekong stole repeatedly into fragments of my life. It was to become more familiar to me than the Thames is to many Londoners. I was in my early twenties, one of six hundred-odd journalists accredited in Saigon to the United States Military Assistance Command Vietnam (MACV) and, in Phnom Penh, one of a much smaller group accredited to the US-backed government of the ill-fated Khmer Republic.

The Mekong soon washed through me like a tide. I learned something about life and death there that I could never have perceived in Europe. I learned about the excitement of the romance, tinged with melancholy, that is so peculiar to this corner of Asia. I learned, too, that the Mekong is not as innocent a river as it sometimes looks. It is true that the Mekong brings life to the lands of Indo-China; but there is another face of it that, in due course, I got

4

to know too well. It is a face that reflects the violence and corruption of the countries it touches.

This was never entirely the sleepy Asian backwater of docile, gently smiling peasants which it was popularly portrayed to be, but a place of despotism, primitive destructiveness and suffering. History has demonstrated that violence as well as sensuous pleasure is intrinsic to the Indo-Chinese character and to Cambodians in particular. Violence is in the blood. Cambodians 'appear only to have known how to destroy, never to reconstruct', wrote Henri Mouhot, the great French explorer who died of jungle fever exploring the upper reaches of the river in 1861. Of the Mekong, he said: 'I have so long drunk of its waters, it has so long either cradled me on its bosom or tried my patience – at one time flowing majestically among the mountains, at another muddy and yellow as the Arno at Florence.'

For myself, there are certain things I shall never forget: the bodies I saw being tossed about in its violent eddies near a ferry town thirty-two miles south of Phnom Penh in the early morning mist when the Mekong is at its most majestic and mysterious; or the dawn tragedy of the B52 bomber of the United States air force which prematurely unleashed its cargo of high-explosives on the same little town, turning its centre into a flattened mass of rubble under which many people lay dead. 'I saw one stick of bombs through the town but it was no great disaster,' Colonel Opfer, the American air attaché, told a press conference. Opfer had not understood a thing. The bombing had killed or wounded some 400 people. One man lost twelve members of his family.

Nor shall I forget the day when a Cambodian general marched his soldiers behind a protective screen of Vietnamese civilians into the waiting guns of the Viet Cong. 'It is a new form of psychological warfare,' the general said as the bodies dropped in front of him.

It was in Phnom Penh, on the banks of one of the *quatre bras* of the Mekong that, one morning in 1975, I thought I was going to die. A young Khmer Rouge soldier put a pistol to my head. There did not seem to be any reason why he would not pull the trigger. Today, I still have the uneasy feeling that perhaps I should not be alive.

Of course there were other sides to these things, too. One can be romantic as well as cynical about war. There can be a magic attraction about tragedy; there can be exhilaration as well as exhaustion. When death is close, every object, every feeling, is golden. Camaraderie is stronger, love is deeper.

Time inevitably dims the intensity of one's feelings. Yet often I have a burning desire to go back to where it all began for me. But not so much the Cambodia I knew at the end, in its most tragic and lonely hour, when Phnom Penh was a city under siege, swathed in barbed wire, swamped by refugees whose suffering presented one of the most haunting images of twentieth century Asia.

I want to go back to the Cambodia of early 1970 and the innocence of my first trip to Indo-China. I dream of Phnom Penh's flower-scented streets; the simplicity of the villages along the banks of the Mekong surrounded by mangoes, bananas and coconuts; the splendour of the jungle; the rice fields green as lawns; the exquisite women; the odour of opium; the warm caress of the heat; and the peace that reigned over it all. The dawning of a beautiful love affair – that too belongs to the Indo-China I cherish.

What carries me back to the Cambodia of my dreams is those first days. On that cold 1970 morning I had left Paris behind me, shuttered and pigeon grey beneath the monotony of a northern sky. I had been working on the English Desk of Agence France-Presse (AFP) for nearly two years, but harboured a desire to be posted to Vietnam and badgered my editors unashamedly to be sent there. My passion for Indo-China was fuelled in part by a brief flirtation with the French Foreign Legion, which had fought with such distinction there, and in part by a zest for adventure, which is why I became a journalist in the first place. In the end, a *coup d'état* was the answer to my prayers. The new rulers regarded Jean Barré, the AFP correspondent in Phnom Penh, as hostile and expelled him. In their wisdom, the French chiefs of AFP decided to replace him with a non-Frenchman. I was their choice and was sent as an envoyé special on a three month assignment. I stayed for five years.

Twenty hours after taking off from Paris, the airplane made a final turn, the Mekong slid into sight then fell sharply away and I landed at Phnom Penh, a different world. On my first day I felt I had entered a beautiful garden. As I stepped off the Air France Boeing 707 onto the hot tarmac of Phnom Penh's Pochentong airport to begin a new life, I forgot about Paris and began an adventure and a love affair with Indo-China to which I have been faithful ever since.

I can still see it all in my mind's eye and sense its indolent charm. Here and there on the road from the little airport where I had been met by Bernard Ullman, a correspondent with AFP, stood trees with astounding red flowers. The rocket attacks and acts of terrorism would not begin for some months and you could walk or be pedalled noiselessly through the streets without danger. There were few cars and, initially, little sign of war. Soldiers went to fight in gaily painted buses and Pepsi-Cola trucks requisitioned by the army.

7

My home was Studio Six, a two bedroom duplex with ceiling fans on the ground floor of the Hôtel Le Royal. This spacious, almost baronial building, wrapped with flaming red bougainvillaea had once been the French Officers' Club and more recently a comfortable base for tourists from France who came to Cambodia for *la chasse*, to visit the temples of Angkor and to savour the legendary beauty of the women. I liked its romantic air at once. Its carved wooden staircase leading to what seemed like miles of dimly lit corridors, the garden lush with strange plants, with a pool at the back, the faded picture of Angkor on its snuff-coloured walls, the machine-gun rattle of French from old rubber planters downing Pernods at the bar.

In the studio there were piles of old copies of *Le Monde*, books, water bottles, rucksacks, cameras, discarded machine-gun bullets and an exotic *Carte Touristique du Cambodge* on the wall, illustrated with images of elephants, tigers, temples, waterfalls, across all of which the serpentine Mekong meandered in a thick blue line.

The city was bathed in a soft and purplish evening light. Bernard, a veteran Asia hand, took me that night to the Café de Paris, Phnom Penh's best French restaurant, to celebrate my arrival. Albert Spaccessi, the fat Corsican proprietor, his loose trousers hitched up with braces under his nipples, greeted us with loud effusiveness and positively glowed with hospitality. We dined on local venison washed down by fine French wines, beneath cheap posters of Nôtre Dame and the Place de la Concorde. But instead of emerging afterwards into a grey Paris street, full of passers-by hurrying with bent heads and collars turned up against the chill, I stepped into an enchanting world of tropical scents, the evening silence broken only by a bevy of girls in their cyclos who crowded round offering to pass the night with us.

That evening, as we were pedalled back to the hotel in a cyclo, Bernard explained how he felt. 'Indo-China is like a beautiful woman; she overwhelms you and you never quite understand why,' he said with unashamed tenderness. 'Sometimes a man can lose his heart to a place, one that lures him back again and again.'

I have never forgotten his words.

War in the Rice Fields

This day was given to myself
for the preparation of leaving . . .
packing uniforms
and one last look,
folding memories neatly inside of myself
and folding underwear into bags . . .
taking only what I need
and hoping that will be enough.

The visions of Cambodia always return – in colours, in people dying, in the dignity of the women toiling in the rice fields, in the glitter of dusk over the Mekong, in the barefoot children playing tag in the streets. Phnom Penh in early 1970 was ravishing: Buddhist monks in saffron robes and shaven heads walking down avenues of blossom-scented trees; schoolgirls in white blouses and blue skirts pedalling past with dazzling smiles, offering garlands of jasmine to have their pictures taken; lovers strolling in the evening along the placid river bank by the old Royal Palace; elephant rides in a park; tinkling bells coming from the shrine on top of the mound from which the city takes its name.

After the bustle of Europe, there was a curious sensation that time stood still. With the coming of the war, this gracious tolerant life did not vanish overnight. Rather, it unravelled gradually like a ball of twine. There was hardly any visible poverty. Life revolved around the family, the Buddhist festivals, the rhythm of the seasons, as it had done since the time of Angkor, the pinnacle of Khmer civilis-ation. These Cambodians were not wily like their quicksilver Thai and Vietnamese neighbours, but pleasure-seeking, insouciant, with a childish faith in the ability of westerners to solve their problems.

13

They lived simply, naturally. They had no idea of the havoc that was to come. Their naïveté was touching. To me, it was an integral part of their charm.

I brought to Phnom Penh next to no clothes but a few books and the usual immutable paraphernalia of the journalist in those days – an Olivetti Lettera 32 portable typewriter and a camera. Going to Indo-China, I felt I was following my deepest instincts, drawn by some inner compulsion. Ever since my teens, this corner of Southeast Asia had seemed to me mysterious and oddly poetic; now here I was in its most enchanting city, able to be myself without being under obligation to anyone for the first time since I had left public school.

I explored the friendly little city – a perfect fusion of French and Asian cultures – feeling I had arrived in a world of new dimensions where all my dreams could come true. All the accumulated restraints of western life could be abandoned in the primitive simplicity and beauty of Indo-China. I'd had a reasonable amount of luck – loving parents, a good education in Britain – but I was determined to make my way as a foreign correspondent without the string-pulling that marked many such careers. Here I would be able to say my goodbyes to the gaucheries of my youthful self and be free for the first time in my life.

I arrived with a young man's conceptions about the glory of war and believing firmly in the chivalrous ideal. I had read widely; I had grown up on Buchan, Conrad, Forester, Henty, Wren, but also on books about World War Two and France's own wars in Indo-China. The need to confront a life-threatening situation was strong. I itched to know, albeit with trepidation, how I would react on the borderland of death. Would I behave like a staunch Buchan hero or panic and run away?

I already had an Indian upbringing which gave me a feel for life in a colonial environment. Until 1953 I grew up in the first years of independent India, but my parents' life was even then pure British colonial. I was much more seduced by the French version, based I believed, in simplistic terms, on the system of the three Bs – Bars, Boulevards and Brothels. Of course there was much more to it than that; and this helped make Indo-China so appealing and intriguing to me when I finally arrived there.

The French backed their colonial ideals by imposing on the natives of Indo-China their own ideas about education, culture and religion. Their rule often turned out to be brutal. But making a comparison of the French and British colonial systems, Lyautey – that enlightened Marshal of France, who had played a heroic part in France's conquest of Tonkin, the northernmost region of Vietnam – once said that the British had the advantage over the French in that the people they sent to the East 'are usually gentlemen'. However, he went on to say: 'We have one over you. We are less exclusive in our contacts with Orientals, and less obsessed by social and colour prejudices.' And it was true. A French army officer walking down the street with his native wife and métis children in tow was commonplace in France's colonies. The English frowned on intermarriage, isolated themselves in 'Whites Only' clubs and tended to regard their colonial subjects as belonging to a lower social order. But in Indo-China, the French colonised down to the very roots of life so that even the poor ferryman on the Mekong might once have been a Frenchman – sometimes the man painting at the top of the ladder and the man holding the bottom of the ladder would both be French. In the hidebound India of the British Raj, an Englishman would never have deigned to such 'lowly' jobs. This difference of approach, French and British, was very evident in Cambodia where, for instance, a French institution like the Lycée Descartes across the tree-lined avenue from Le Royal was, when I arrived, a delightful racial mixture of walnut-brown Cambodian and white French children.

Le Royal soon became home, its courteous staff under Monsieur Loup, the *patron*, as familiar as my colleagues. It was also a place where the foreign community, particularly the French, congregated. Each day saw long-legged French girls grace the pool. Their presence conjured up an irresistible atmosphere of hot sex and ice-cold drinks. La Sirène, the outdoor restaurant, served fresh Kep lobster, crab and delicious fish called Les Demoiselles du Mekong. A permanent fixture was a bronzed bald-headed and muscular Frenchman who swam fifty lengths of the pool first thing in the morning. He was Doctor Paul Grauwin, who as the médecin-chef at the siege of Dien Bien Phu in 1954 was one of the heroes of that terrible battle which lost France its Asian empire. This modest hero had made Phnom Penh his home and ran a medical clinic in the town.

The westerners – particularly many of the 3000-strong French community – were inured to the fighting; indeed, the war added a certain *frisson* to lives spent in cosy white villas behind high walls. The French had, on the whole, a healthy distrust of journalists, most of whom were Americans, and they received them dubiously, sometimes with overt hostility. They associated them with bad news and chaos; and in a sense they were right to do so. These Frenchmen believed that the communists were winning the war in Vietnam, not just because of the failings of the United States army, with its bad habit of substituting firepower for manpower, but also as a result of the wide access to the battlefield that the US accorded to journalists.

They chose to forget that the French, too, had lost their own war in Indo-China, despite the heavy restrictions they had placed on the movement of members of the press. Accordingly, they tended to be stand-offish and to resent the intrusion of Anglo-Saxon journalists into their territory. It was difficult to argue with them for they had been living in a haven of peace. And now their comfortable world was fragmenting as the Vietnam war spilled across the borders into this exotic backwater. Some of the French, particularly the rubber-planters, who had previously lived in Vietnam, were seeing their agony unfold all over again.

Before 1970, few countries in Asia were so united by their leaders as Cambodia was behind Prince Norodom Sihanouk. His little kingdom was still a marvellous oasis of peace. It was a deceptive calm, however. Parts of the peasantry had been radicalised by the years of resistance against the French. There was a deep-rooted dislike among them for anyone and anything to do with the towns, which they saw as the fount of corruption and oppression. These stirrings of rural discontent finally boiled over into a peasant uprising in northwestern Cambodia which Sihanouk's army crushed ruthlessly.

By now Cambodia's neutrality was heavily qualified; it was being tragically abused by both the Vietnamese communists and the Americans. The port of Kompong Som (in those days called Sihanoukville) was the entry point for military supplies from North Vietnam transported through Cambodia to the communist forces in South Vietnam. In 1969 President Nixon authorised the savage and secret B52 bombing of the sanctuaries of the Viet Cong and North Vietnamese communists just inside Cambodia's borders with South Vietnam,

17

less than seventy miles from Phnom Penh. The dream of Cambodian neutrality dissolved.

In March 1970, while Sihanouk was abroad, he fell victim to a *coup d'état* organised by his right-wing Minister of Defence, General Lon Nol, which deprived him of his position as Head of State for Life. Petulantly, he allied himself with his enemies, the tiny group of Cambodian communists known as the Khmer Rouge whom he had previously sought to destroy, and with Ho Chi Minh and the communists of Hanoi. Lon Nol took Cambodia into the Vietnam war on the side of South Vietnam and the United States, and that was the beginning of disaster. The unity of Cambodia disintegrated in a bitter, inglorious war. Five years of carnage were followed by bloody revolution, famine and foreign occupation. The aftershocks are being felt to this day.

Lon Nol gave the Vietnamese communist forces forty-eight hours to leave. They ignored him. A wave of anti-Vietnamese sentiment swept the country, reflecting the deep, ages-old enmity between the two ethnically and culturally distinct peoples. It was cynically stirred up by the Lon Nol government.

Thousands of Vietnamese whose families had lived in Phnom Penh for years, even generations, sheltered in improvised camps, in churches, in schools, for protection from Cambodian anger. Upcountry, thousands more Vietnamese men and women were massacred, their bodies cast into the Mekong to float downstream past Phnom Penh and Neak Leung. A French Roman Catholic priest stood by his mission on the banks of the Mekong day and night, weeping and trying to count the bodies. Soon afterwards, his throat was slit by the communist guerrillas.

By the time I arrived, the irrationality of the war was already apparent. Lon Nol, the coup leader, was emerging as a weak vassal. His American patrons were incapable or unwilling to control the corruption, waste and incompetence of his army commanders. The army was outgeneralled by the Vietnamese communists. A combined American and South Vietnamese drive into eastern Cambodia to destroy the North Vietnamese (NVA) and Viet Cong sanctuaries helped protect the US withdrawal from South Vietnam but was a disaster for Cambodia. The war spread across the land as the NVA were driven from the border areas and melted deeper into the interior of the country for security. One by one, the provinces fell to them and their Cambodian communist allies, the Khmer Rouge, or became totally insecure. In no time at all, Phnom Penh was cut off from much of the countryside and there was often skirmishing on its outer perimeter.

Though they were looking into the abyss of civil war, the Cambodians retained a sense of fun. On Proclamation of Republic Day in October 1970, when the Lon Nol government formally abolished the monarchy, Phnom Penh seethed with life. There were fairs everywhere and the city exuded a sense of continual and mischievous rejoicing. Food was not exorbitantly priced; the pavements were not yet the long dormitories of sleeping people they were later to become; the cafés were full; the milling crowds were smiling and gentle-eyed; the very air they breathed seemed to ring with laughter. Phnom Penh was an abidingly pretty city; absurd as it would later seem, its people were then filled with hope.

In a corner of my studio at the Hôtel Le Royal stood a mysterious rucksack and a camera bag. They had been there for some time; unclaimed, forlorn and seemingly forgotten. Often I wondered about the owner. One day I asked my colleagues and was told they belonged to a handsome young French photographer, Claude Arpin, who had gone missing in eastern Cambodia a few days before my arrival. I soon learned that Arpin was one of a whole group of journalists of all nationalities who had disappeared in the chaotic first days of the war, when there were no front lines and a road that was secure in the morning often changed hands without warning in the course of the day.

Among them were two Frenchmen: Guy Hannoteau, a writer I had met in Chad six months before and whose intelligence and sense of adventure I greatly admired; and Gilles Caron, who had made his name as a brilliant action photographer in the 1968 Paris riots. Sean Flynn, the photographer son of Errol, enticed back from a holiday in Bali by the outbreak of the Cambodian war, had also vanished down the same road. Two decades later, they are still missing. Proportionally more journalists were to lose their lives in Cambodia in those early, desperately dangerous weeks of the war than in any other conflict since World War Two.

I never met Arpin. He was captured and is presumed dead, though nobody quite knows precisely how he was killed. But over the next few years I felt his shadow. He was the apotheosis of those young French men of action in the difficult post-war years who were prepared to risk their lives for their beliefs. It was as if they felt a burning need to assuage France's shame of her 1940 defeat and the Occupation by deliberately seeking tests of skill and courage under the skies of Indo-China and North Africa. A former soldier in the French colonial paratroops who by conviction had supported the cause of Algérie Française and had been imprisoned for his role in the army revolt against Général de Gaulle, he had come to Vietnam to become a war photographer. He was an angry man, at odds with France's de-colonising period. Like the others, he was lost one hot day on Highway One, looking for a battle to photograph.

Highway One, the old Route Coloniale, runs parallel with the Mekong from Phnom Penh down to the ferry crossing of Neak Leung, then on through the rice-rich province of Svay Rieng to the Vietnamese border to Saigon. Ordinarily, it was a journey of no special moment. But it was on this road beside the Mekong where so many journalists were taken prisoner, that some of the bloodiest early engagements of the war were fought, and where I first experienced being under fire.

The advance of the Vietnamese communists from their sanctuaries in eastern Cambodia had brought their columns to within fifteen miles of the eastern suburbs of Phnom Penh. Now the Cambodian army, under General Dien Del – perhaps its best general, a man with a merry sparkle in his eyes and a lovely wife – was mounting an advance to roll them back. Dien Del had set up his headquarters in a pagoda on the Mekong river bank. Frustrated at having to cover the war from the daily military communiqués issued by the High Command spokesman, Major Am Rong (an unfortunate name in the circumstances), whose favourite phrase was 'Aucun incident significatif', I was chafing to go out into the field. Bernard agreed, provided I could get a lift with a battle-seasoned correspondent who would keep an eye on an enthusiastic newcomer and make sure my eagerness did not become a liability.

We set off in the afternoon and, as it became too late and dangerous to drive the short distance back to Phnom Penh, we spent the night in a white pagoda under the eyes of the thoughtful Buddha.

Tiny lights darted outside, fireflies among the trees. Children like little burnt almonds appeared from nowhere, their eyes wide with wonder at the sight of a group of long-nosed strangers. We slept on the floor. The night was hot and tense; the mosquitoes came in clouds. Dawn was on its way when I awoke. The horizon over the Mekong was streaked with red. We splashed ourselves with river water and wondered what the day would hold. Dien Del gave orders for the advance and his troops moved down in single file on each side of the narrow road, backed by a couple of half-track personnel carriers. We followed, while the children and their mothers stared bleakly after us. Dien Del's intention was to reach Neak Leung that evening. The soldiers were in gym shoes, grenades hanging like apples from their belts, and lugging bundles of rice. Most shouldered AK47s, the weapons of the Viet Cong, and some had Mat49s, French machine-pistols. As a talisman, they wore on a string around their necks a carved ivory image of the Buddha to deflect the bullets. For many, as for me, it was to be our *baptême du feu*. For what seemed an eternity but was actually only a couple of hours we moved down the road. Sunlight filtered through the trees. The road was lonely, but the soldiers walked nonchalantly, while I felt a mounting anticipation and excitement. Much of their training had been conducted by the French military mission in Phnom Penh, but they showed a singular lack of military precision as they ambled along the road.

22

The only visible signs of the war were the blackened spars of houses burnt down in earlier fighting. The ambush came suddenly, scattering troops in all directions. One moment there was stillness. Then there was a burst of noise and confusion. A 75mm recoilless rifle opened fire from the brush beside the road. There was a boom and shudder of air. Guns spat around us. I dived behind a tree. There was shooting all around me now and it no longer mattered where it came from. It was close and it hammered at the brain. The tree I crouched behind seemed suddenly wafer thin.

For more than an hour, the battle swirled to and fro. The Viet Cong had spotted us and the earth nearby rose in little spurts. Then, without warning, the gunfire subsided. The Viet Cong had pulled back. There had been only a few of them, a suicide squad left to block the Cambodians' advance, to give the main VC force time to complete its withdrawal. The story spread that they were chained to their weapons to ensure they would fight to the death. It was nonsense. They were highly motivated, deadly soldiers; one could not help but admire their courage, if not their ideology.

This was my first brush with death. An intense physical exhilaration swept through me at still being alive. Our advance took us down to the river bank of the Mekong and I stripped off and plunged in, the first of many cleansing dips in the great river. I savoured the coolness of the water, then walked back along the bank to the car. I tripped over the body of a dead Cambodian soldier and inquisitiveness got the better of revulsion. I lingered beside the corpse, puzzled at the look of composure and serenity on the young man's face and the dark stains on the olive-green uniform. All the time, the Mekong was sliding by, a powerful but paradoxical image of tranquillity. I never knew the dead soldier's name, but I thought afterwards about

23

this human debris in the field and suddenly realised I had turned a corner in my life; in an important sense, I had come of age. I remembered the warning from my godfather, who had won an MC with the Eighth Army in North Africa, that the most dangerous time in war was nearly always the first few weeks. The newcomer was prone to inordinate risk-taking, convinced he was invincible, certain that the bullets that split the air were always intended for someone else. No two trees are quite alike, and for years I could remember precisely the rain-tree with its spreading branches behind which I hid on that clear, hot May day. It was later felled on the orders of the Khmer Rouge, who had the entire avenue of trees along Highway One cut down for firewood, at the same time preventing the peasants from using them as shade from the hot glare of the sun. This destruction caused large parts of the road to cave in through soil erosion.

The front was close to Phnom Penh; so close indeed that a thirty-minute drive in almost any direction provided a grandstand view of the war. Journalists could ride out, catch an unpleasant whiff of cordite in their nostrils and be back at Le Royal for breakfast by the pool. Indeed, it took less time to get to the front line than a Londoner takes to drive to work through the morning rush-hour traffic.

The days were not always eventful. I even found time to start Cambodian language lessons. Somehow, my progress was sadly limited to the Cambodian proverb, '*Mean touk mean trey, mean luy mean srey*' ('Where there is water there are fishes, where there is money there are women'), which was always greeted with smiles which broke the ice.

24

But it was on one of those morning sorties that I felt the jagged edge of fear and saw the war in all its misery and waste. The Viet Cong had cut off the road from Phnom Penh to the provincial town of Takeo. The Cambodian army was trying to reopen it, as it did almost every morning. Villagers told the commander of the little task force that the Viet Cong were dug in at the village of Tran Knar just up ahead. The dyke road rose several feet above the rice fields, so advancing troops had little or no cover from the men lying in ambush in their bunkers. Here, in the myopic tradition of World War One, the Cambodian advance was led by a standard bearer, a boy of seventeen with overlong hair, whose sum knowledge of military matters was three days token training at a recruiting depot before his dispatch to the front. Bravely, he marched ten paces ahead, his battalion's flag born triumphantly aloft as he had been instructed to do on parade. He marched straight into the waiting guns of the Viet Cong. The air crackled with gunfire and the boy's body leaped into the air as if it had been hit by a truck and fell in a crumpled heap on the tarmac. As the soldiers scattered, the major who had given him the job turned away, ashamed to show his grief in front of his men. Bullets cracked through the air and pinged off the road but the major did not seem to notice. He ordered two stretcher-bearers to recover the dead boy and the yellow flag at his side. They scampered up the bank onto the road under covering fire from the others, half-scooped and half-pulled the body and the blood-splashed flag off the road and scurried like beaten dogs to safety.

When the boy died, I was in the middle of a paddy field 200 yards to the right, alone and too frightened to move. The Viet Cong kept on firing. The bullets ripped through the low mudbank and the straggly bush behind which I was hiding. It was clear I was at this moment a prime target and it would have been fatal to stay. I started to crawl. It seemed to take an age. In the end I got up and ran. The field was naked and open. I bent low, heart pounding, and darted across, expecting the impact of a bullet at any moment. When, by some miracle, I reached a muddy ditch, I tried to light a Gauloise but I could not hold the lighter. Meanwhile, the major seemed to lead a charmed life. He was fearless, standing on the road above, directing the battle. To my left, a young soldier hid his head under a waterproof cover, put his Buddha talisman between his teeth for protection, and sobbed in terror. The major came over and kicked him to his feet. Then the Viet Cong blew up the Cambodians' armoured car with a B40 rocket. As smoke and flames poured out of it, three Cambodians leapt out of the turret, their uniforms on fire, screaming in pain and jumped into the waterlogged field to douse the flames. The water hissed around them. By the time the battle was over, the village was blazing. Eight Cambodians were killed and 20 wounded. No Viet Cong bodies were found. It was another of those dirty little battles that made up the war, and in the general scheme of things was an insignificant incident. But I could not forget my own fear, the image of the boy soldier crumpled in the dust and the major who turned his face away and wept.

There was an endearing bravado about Cambodian officers. One general, Um Savath, had got drunk one night, placed an empty Nestlé milk tin on his head and with a superb sense of showmanship ordered his batman to shoot it off. The batman raised his rifle and fired. He was trembling so much that he missed. The bullet hit Um Savath in the head. He was brain-damaged and partially paralysed. Until his death, later on in the Cambodian war, he walked with a limp. He was mad, but insanely brave; his soldiers worshipped him.

*

All this exposure to danger began to be routine. I did not want to become hardened to the bloodshed, but inevitably there were times when I had to be, in order to survive. There were reporters who hardly seemed to care; perhaps, for most, it was just that they knew that if they allowed themselves to give free rein to their feelings they could not have continued to do their job. Soon after daybreak we would foray into the countryside and witness the fighting, see the maimed and mutilated. Then we would drive back to Phnom Penh. Reaching the hotel was a moment of authentic joy. As the gates opened and the car turned into the driveway, we knew we were safe. War is a kind of jailbreak which we welcomed for its freedoms and its lifting of every kind of taboo. In time, there seemed to be no other reality but battle interspersed with relapses of agreeable apathy in Phnom Penh, and the familiarity of those homecomings to our hotel was a precious thing.

The eternal Mekong, gliding by the city on its way to the sea, provided some of the more bizarre distractions. On Sundays after Mass at Phnom Penh's Roman Catholic cathedral – later dynamited by the Khmer Rouge – some French people went water-skiing on its safer stretches, while Cambodian gunboats provided them with protection. This led to its own kind of tragedy when a French girl was cut to ribbons by a boat's propeller. Wartime is the time to do wild things; another form of relaxation could be found in the company of the girls at the *maisons flottantes*, bordering the river a few miles outside Phnom Penh or with the cyclo-girls who congregated outside the Café de Paris. There were opium parlours and Madame Nam's, a brothel specialising in *caresses délicieuses*. The journalist Donald Wise said he once spotted a sign on a doorway saying

'Cunnilingus is spoken here'. One establishment whose location was a jealously guarded secret of the French *colons* refined this art by training its girls first on bananas. Sex and opium played important parts in our lives in Cambodia; these diversions were an essential ingredient of survival.

The wartime capital encouraged all kinds of indiscretions. It had its own resident French lady of pleasure, like a small town in Provence: Madame Cha-Cha, red-bonneted, face caked with coarse make-up, was a grotesque figure compared to the graceful Asian girls who almost floated down the streets. She had had a chequered history, beginning as a *pute* in the rue Saint-Denis, graduating to Marseilles, then to Algeria and finally serving the French Corps Expéditionnaire in Indo-China. Who knows why she stayed? Perhaps out of sentiment. In any case, she was a favourite with Cambodian army officers who regarded her as a stalwart specimen of French womanhood.

Venereal disease was rife, and one or two clinics treated it to the exclusion of almost every other disease. Obsolete treatments, dating back to the French army days and involving courses of mercury, were still in use. 'Be prudent,' Doctor Grauwin advised. 'Always take precautions. Remember the old saying we had in the Corps Expéditionnaire. "Three minutes with Venus is three years with mercury." ' Even so, the press corps went down like flies; one unfortunate colleague was afflicted eleven times.

Jean-Pierre Martini was a young French mathematics professor who taught at Phnom Penh university as a *coopérant*, an alternative to Service Militaire. An habitué of Studio Six, he was a Maoist at heart, believing in permanent revolution. He had a wonderfully warped view of life. His Paris 1968 background had convinced him of the righteousness of the communist cause in Cambodia. However

28

Jean-Pierre's number one passion was not politics but voyeurism. He used to regale me with stories of his sexual exploits and experiments with Cambodian girls, and seemed to be in a state of perpetual adolescence. It was he who made the interesting observation that the borderline between Cambodia and Vietnam is also the boundary of the female *labia majora*; on the Cambodian side women's genitalia are more often fully developed as a result of their Indian heritage, but in Vietnam and further eastwards they are small and shell-like in the Mongoloid tradition.

Once, he returned from a visit to Phnom Penh Central Market with the perfectly formed rim of the eye of a deer he had spotted at a stall of Cambodian folk medicine where they also sold tigers' teeth and the bile of cobras. He explained, with a flourish, that Cambodian men liked to stick it on the end of their penis like a 'tickler' to excite their partner better during intercourse. No woman, regardless of her looks, was spared his advances. There was a secretary at the New Zealand embassy whom we called Pinched Lips because of her pursed unsmiling mouth. One of Jean-Pierre's maxims was that it was not a woman's looks that mattered when making love, it was her 'technique'; if that was good, she gave pleasure even if she was plug-ugly. One afternoon, he arrived in the studio, a little out of breath, eyes sparkling with mischief, to announce. 'Je l'ai baisé.' What was it like, I asked. 'C'était formidable!' he cried. 'C'était la Technique Commonwealth!'

While the French got on with their lives and the Cambodians, Chinese and remnants of the frightened Vietnamese community muddled through and made contingency plans for their future, a dangerous competitive streak developed among the press corps. They were in a mood to despise danger and allow the narrowest possible margin of safety. Courage became a cult. More and more journalists went down uncannily empty roads never to return – twenty in a few weeks – and then one day I myself pushed my luck too hard. In southwest Cambodia beyond the infamous Pich Nil pass, close by the Gulf of Siam, I was so desperate to glimpse the sea, to feel its wet air on my face, that I broke my rule never to be on the roads after four in the afternoon, when it begins to grow dark and the peasants leave their fields.

Faced with the choice of spending a lonely night at a Cambodian outpost guarding a bridge about fifty miles from Phnom Penh, which was quite likely to be attacked and overrun, or of driving with all speed to the next provincial town, Kompong Speu, I chanced it and chose the latter. I drove recklessly without headlights, leaning tensely forward, peering into the gloom. The Peugeot 404 crashed into a mine-crater, turned over and skidded for yards on its side before coming to a halt, a wreck. Scrambling out through the shattered windscreen, with a gashed shoulder, I spent a terrifying night in the rice fields, expecting capture at any moment.

It was a beautiful tropical night; the stars shone like crystal – but this was no time to admire them. The area was a major Khmer Rouge supply and infiltration route to the Seven Mountains, and above the croak of bullfrogs and the rasp of cicadas I could hear the groaning of ox-carts carrying ammunition; ox-carts of the same design as those on the murals at Angkor Wat. The very darkness seemed to hold its breath; at each sound my muscles tightened in anticipation of a bullet. I even believed I could hear the Khmer Rouge breathing. Dawn brought the chirp of birds and villagers driving their grey buffalo to the fields. An army patrol came down

30

the road in search of what it expected to be a body. I was bleary-eyed but safe, though I richly deserved not to be. Never again did I break the four o'clock code or take insane risks. Indeed, for years afterwards I was nervous about driving in the dark in Asia, once breaking out in a cold sweat driving through the rubber plantations of Malaysia at dusk, looking for a place to hide and having to stop the car to recover my nerve.

In place of the Peugeot, a total write-off, I rented a little Japanese sports car. It roared like a Panzer Division on the move but I felt safer close to the ground. People usually shoot high in split-second ambushes. One memorable day, I took my colleague Donald Wise on an expedition to the front and we ended up having a picnic in a field – a bottle of Beaujolais, smoked oysters and a baguette – protected by a Cambodian paratroop battalion consisting entirely of girl soldiers. Mortars rasped and popped not far away but I felt safe. The presence of the girls certainly slowed down our lunch. We beat a retreat when a mortar bomb stuck in its tube and the mortar team, with typical Khmer insouciance, turned the tube upside down to shake it out. But never since have I had the benefit of such a charmingly coquettish, protective shield.

Such times were all very pleasant. They could not last. Buried somewhere among the reefs of my mind is still the memory of a sultry Phnom Penh afternoon. The Khemara cinema in the Avenue Charles de Gaulle was comfortably filled. There were some soldiers in uniforms. There were many women and children. It seemed like any other afternoon at the pictures. The film was *Enfer sur les Philippines*, an American film about the battle of Bataan, dubbed in French.

31

It was very quiet in the third-floor flat opposite. I had dropped by for a siesta with Mademoiselle Hoa, a half-Cambodian, half-Vietnamese girl with a cat's beauty and midnight blue-black hair. We used to smoke opium together. The drowsy sleep it produced was the perfect antidote to a day at the front. Now, as we lay in the clammy air in her bedroom I wondered, not for the first time, whether I would ever be able to tear myself away from Indo-China.

Then came an unmistakable noise – a dull boom from across the street which ended the steamy rêverie. No one spoke. Hoa's flirtatious eyes filled with fear and she gripped my hand like a frightened child. I looked out of the window. People were tumbling out of the cinema and falling, in slow motion, to the ground. Someone had thrown a couple of grenades inside and they had burst in the air and showered the audience with splinters.

I was gripped by a mixture of curiosity and horror. I remember dressing and rushing across the road. Inside the cinema, the air was thick with blood and death. There was whimpering from rows of broken bodies and wet red stains on the floor gleaming in the faint light. There was a little girl who still breathed but whose body was full of grenade fragments and who clenched a peanut between her front teeth as if her life depended on it.

I carried her into the street and laid her gently on the ground, then went back in. When I returned she was still there, an innocent child close to death. All around was pandemonium, military police waving guns, but not a single ambulance. As a community, Phnom Penh was not organised to deal with such a tragedy. Even today, after years of suffering, the Cambodians do not have a strong sense of caring for their fellow men. Medical staff, negligent and greedy, demand to be paid for drugs provided free of charge by the international aid agencies. Perhaps this is due to the Cambodians' fatalistic perception of human life. Perhaps it is due to penury, to the horrors of war that have blighted their lives. For many, morality is a luxury to be disowned; survival and money are the ultimate objectives.

It was left to an American and myself to carry out the wounded. I bent over the girl. She whimpered and twisted as if to shake off death. In desperation I scooped up her broken body and put her in the front of the car, another two wounded in the back seat, another across the open boot, and drove to the military hospital.

The sentry refused to open the gates. Civilian casualties were not allowed in the military hospital. I implored. He shook his head, unmoved. I drove to the Soviet-Khmer friendship hospital on the other side of town, ran inside and grabbed a doctor. My hand, sticky with the girl's blood, marked the sleeve of his white coat. 'If you don't look after these wounded, I will leave them in the courtyard and you will be responsible,' I said. Reluctantly, he called for orderlies to unload the car. I took a last look at the child. Her mouth opened in a silent plea for help and for an instant her tiny fingers touched my hand. Then she was gone.

In the morning, I went back. The child was dead. Her name did not matter. She was very young and had committed no crime. Twenty-three people were killed that afternoon by the hand grenades. Few died outright. It was a small thing when every day scores were dying in the great greenness of the Cambodian countryside, but the sense of waste was overwhelming. Seldom has the ending of a little life so touched me.

By the following morning the bloodstains had been washed away. The military police closed all Phnom Penh's cinemas and fleshpots and said they would punish the criminals. But who were the criminals? Most probably angry soldiers who had not been paid. Three weeks later, the Khemara reopened to *La Chanson de Demain*, a Shaw Brothers of Hong Kong romance. The earlier killing might never have happened. The whole incident had disappeared into thin air.

Herein lay a recurring dilemma: in what circumstances should a journalist stop being a journalist and intervene to save lives? As I have said, there were some reporters who hardly seemed to care, developing a detached attitude to death. Perhaps they had found that personal involvement brought only pain and so masked their feelings with an outward display of hardened professionalism. Were they right? It was hard to think so. Yet on this occasion I was so preoccupied with the wounded that I was the last to file a story. My story was strong on colour and detail, but it was hopelessly late and I got a rocket from AFP in Paris. The editors there had, however, appreciated my difficulties and my dilemma. At the end of their note they added a single French word – *'Courage'*.

By late 1970, Cambodia was becoming a country without a future. The cream of Lon Nol's army had been defeated in an ill-conceived offensive named Chenla, after the pre-Angkorian kingdom of the same name. The twenty battalions of the task force were bogged down on Highway Six, linking Phnom Penh with the provincial capital of Kompong Thom. Strung out for several miles along the narrow asphalt road, the Cambodians were an easy prey for the Vietnamese lying in wait in the surrounding fields and rubber plantations. They were cut to pieces by the communists' heavy guns and their forces never reached the besieged town; its inhabitants were reduced to eating the animals in their picturesque little zoo to stay alive. The Cambodians never recovered from this blow. Early in 1971, Lon Nol suffered a stroke. Although his health improved, he was never in full political control again. He became a recluse, surrounding himself with Buddhist monks, genuflecting fortune-tellers and clanging gongs in the palace of Chamcar Mon. There was to be no magic solution to this war.

In those hard-bitten days, a number of us smoked opium. It seemed natural to do so after a day at the front. Opium had been legal in Indo-China just a few years before, and while it was now officially prohibited, was still widely smoked among the French *colons*. The most famous *fumerie* in Phnom Penh was Madame Chum's. Madame Chum, a one-time mistress of a former president of the national assembly, was Cambodia's Opium Queen. She ran the *fumerie* for more than thirty years, until her death in September 1970, aged sixty-seven, and earned a small fortune from the pipe-dreams of others.

Madame Chum sent her two children, a boy and a girl, to France to be educated. She also adopted a host of abandoned Cambodian children as her own, paying for their food, housing and education from her profits. Her generosity made her as well known for welfare work as for opium and she was accorded a national funeral, her body wrapped in a white cloth, holding three lotus flowers as an offering to the Buddha. People said she had never forgotten how she suffered when she was young and poor and had made a vow to help others all she could. I wrote her obituary for AFP and was pleased when *Le Figaro* published it in full.

Her *fumerie*, in a residential part of town near the Independence Monument, was used mainly by the French. They were jealously protective of it and resented other westerners smoking there. When it was briefly closed at the outbreak of war by the authorities, one of the women who worked for Madame Chum decided to do away with the friction this resentment had caused and opened her own den. Her name was Chantal.

The den was called 482 after the side street in which her wooden house on stilts was located. To reach it we pedalled by cyclo through the curfew-stilled streets, past the road checks, past the soldiers lounging at street corners, past the snapping dogs. We pedalled down the centre of the road, afraid that the sentries might shoot us in the darkness. Chantal's first three clients were Kate Webb, a journalist, Kent Potter, a courageous young British photographer, and myself. Our pictures were pinned to the wall; we were part of her family. Chantal was a beautiful woman, soft, smooth and round like a plum. We adored her.

Her house was partitioned into four rooms. Naked except for a sarong, we lay on the coconut-matting covering the bare wooden boards and smoked. Sometimes we had female company. Sometimes we had a traditional Cambodian massage. Sometimes we just talked among ourselves, reminiscing and reflecting on the adventures of the day. Often, one of us would launch into an impassioned soliloquy about the war. One recurring theme was who was the greatest war photographer – the late Robert Capa, Larry Burrows or Don McCullin?

There was a lot of common ground as to why we were in Cambodia. With opium, our inner thoughts took wings. And it turned out that for most of us the enemy was not the deadly carnage in the

Cambodian fields but the tedium of life itself; especially the perceived dreariness and conformity we had left behind in the West, to whose taboos and musty restrictions we dreaded having one day to return. During the day we might have experienced terrifying incidents and made life-and-death decisions as to where to go, and how long it was wise to stay on a battlefield. But the war also provided us with a certain freedom, which is why we liked being here. We felt we had broken loose and were accomplices in an escape from the straitjacket of ease and staid habits.

Lying down and smoking, eyes closed, we were scarcely aware of the outside, even when, through the open window, an occasional flash and boom of artillery reminded us of the battles raging in the countryside. Later on, when the American B52 carpet-bombing came closer to Phnom Penh, we would feel a sullen rolling vibration as though we were on the periphery of a great earthquake. The whole house quivered. Yet, thanks to the soothing balm of the opium, I recall a strange, almost childlike, satisfaction, a feeling of absolute content in the mysterious certainty that we were utterly secure where we lay. Then at some stage, at two or so in the morning, our thoughts drifted away and we sank into an ocean of forgetfulness. Time did not exist in the limbo of the *fumerie*.

Graham Greene, in *Ways of Escape*, said of the four winters he spent in Indo-China, it was opium which 'left the happiest memory', and I understand what he means. I took opium many times in Cambodia. It was sweet and left a lingering acrid fragrance on the palate. The ritual was seductive. I remember very well the old man who made us our pipes. He was spare and the skin on his face was wrinkled like *crêpe*. With a metal spike, he turned a small sizzling ball of sticky opium paste the size of his fingertip over and over in

37

the flame of a little oil-lamp until it was cooked; then he inserted it into the ivory pipe and handed the pipe to me. Little bluish clouds puffed as I drew on it. There were no great visions; just disembodied contentment. It brought tranquillity to the mind and spirit as we lay cocooned in this sanctuary Chantal had created for us in the intimacy of her home.

All manner of people visited her *fumerie* – French planters and their Cambodian mistresses, Frenchwomen and their lovers, diplomats, journalists, spies. None stranger, perhaps, than Igor, the resident Tass correspondent. Igor was an important KGB officer in Phnom Penh, a product of the new generation of sophisticated young Soviet spies who graduated from the Moscow spy school. A natty dresser with well-cut suits and wide flowery Italian ties, he spoke Cambodian and French. He cultivated the western press and was a good friend of Jean-Pierre Martini. But no one had ever seen him commit an indiscretion. He was too much of a professional. It became something of a challenge to get Igor drunk or, better still, into the opium parlour. Even when his skin was full of a fearsome concoction of vodka mixed with marijuana, a creation of some American journalists, he remained as solid as a rock. I have seldom found a drink more corrosive. The Americans loved it. And unlike them, Igor could take it.

On New Year's Eve 1970, Jean-Pierre and Igor organised a joint party. Jean-Pierre offered the champagne, I offered a tin of caviar saved from a stopover at Tehran airport, and Igor provided the food and vodka. Indicative of his rank and the respect in which he was held by the embassy was that he was given the Soviet ambassador's personal chef for the evening. There followed a memorable Georgian meal of meat skewered on swords, roasted and flambéed, washed down with much vodka and champagne. Afterwards, Igor drove me back to the studio at Le Royal. I proposed a visit to Chantal's. To my astonishment and delight, he accepted. Now, I thought, perhaps I can tickle some of those KGB secrets out of him. It was not to be. We each smoked a pipe and passed out on the mat. In the morning when I awoke, Igor had vanished.

The little street 482 is still there near the old petrol station and the heinous Khmer Rouge concentration camp at Tuol Sleng. Years afterwards, I went back. The house had been torn down and there was no trace of Chantal. Had she somehow survived the Khmer Rouge purges and made it to a refugee camp in Thailand and perhaps on to France? Or did she succumb? She had simply vanished. It was almost as if she had never existed.

At times, I would drive a little way out of Phnom Penh and sit by the banks of the great river at Koki. Or visit a Cambodian home and sit on the floor sipping bitter unsweetened tea out of tiny porcelain cups. Dawn was the best time. The countryside was cool and fresh, the air less heavy. A smell of woodsmoke hung in the air, and the water was touched by the first rays of sun. It was almost impossible to imagine that these peasants lived so close to insecurity. But their lives, which had not changed very much over the centuries, were changing now.

The insurgents were often entrenched on the opposite bank of the Mekong. One August day, I sat and watched a Cambodian gunboat shell a Roman Catholic church which the guerrillas were using as a temporary headquarters. A few hours earlier, Spiro Agnew, the soon-to-be-disgraced US Vice-President, had visited the city on a morale-boosting tour. He presented Lon Nol with a baby white elephant, venerated as a sacred symbol of good fortune. In the circumstances, it was an absurd gesture. As the gunboat, anchored in the middle of the flood-swollen river, blasted the church, I watched two men, in khaki, break free of the building and run through the banana grove.

Who were these mysterious insurgents? Were they the same people as this placid and virtuous old peasant man I was sipping tea with, while the women washed clothes and his children frolicked in the water? I often wondered what motivated them. And then one day I got the chance to find out.

Kompong Cham, the main Mekong river port upstream from Phnom Penh – where Cambodia's rubber is loaded for shipment down to the processing factory in the capital – had been the scene of heavy fighting. The Vietnamese communists had captured it early in the war. A South Vietnamese army taskforce, under General Do Cao Tri (later to be killed in a helicopter crash with his passenger, François Sully of *Newsweek*), recaptured it. When I arrived, a volcanic smoke plume was rising over the university on the city's edge. The ripped-apart bodies of women and children accidentally caught in a South Vietnamese bombing raid lay scattered in the road, 'collateral damage' in the vernacular of the war. Down by the river at the command post, Major Ros Proeung of the Cambodian army asked if I wanted to see the prisoners.

He pushed open a door to a tiny room which gave off a smell of raw meat like a slaughterhouse. Two wounded men lay on the floor, their hands bound with wire behind their backs. Their coarse olive-green uniforms were caked in a mixture of mud and blood. They were terribly mutilated, in agony, whimpering like animals in a trap. Suddenly, aware of a foreign presence, they stirred, opened their eyes and looked at me in the dim light. The look on their faces was one of intense hatred. Their eyes burned with loathing. I turned away, sickened by the spectacle. The Major jabbed their wounds with his stick.

'What will happen to them?' I asked. The Major did not answer. I offered to take them to hospital. The Major was irritated, angry. 'Let them die,' he said in a hard voice. 'They are Vietnamese. We did not invite them to come to our country.' And he struck the bodies again and spat on the ground.

Afterwards, I looked through their papers. There was a diary in spidery writing, a little notebook with a faded photograph of Ho Chi Minh, North Vietnam's late President and revolutionary hero, pressed between the pages. It belonged to Lieutenant Dao An Tuat of the North Vietnamese army, one of a whole generation who had never known a real day of peace. Tuat wrote:

> To live is to give oneself to the fatherland,
> It is to give oneself to the earth, the mountains and to the rivers
> It is to clench one's teeth in the face of the enemy,
> To live is to keep up one's courage in times of misery,
> It is to laugh in times of anger,
> To live is to remain optimistic in the struggle,
> It is to crush, it is to break the image of the enemy,
> One must drink passionately of the blood of the enemy.

True to his words, Lieutenant Tuat died in that stinking hole, clenching his teeth 'in the face of the enemy'. The Cambodians took him and his companion down to the riverbank, poured petrol over their bodies and lit a match. Thus the Mekong became a funeral river like the Ganges.

Tuat was one of Uncle Ho's 'children'. Four years before, he had answered the famous slogan that 'nothing is more precious than independence and freedom', and quit his peasant home in North Vietnam to fight for the 'liberation' of South Vietnam. I imagined his long night marches down the Ho Chi Minh trail under the illumination flares, the malaria, the damp-sweats, the terror of the constant bombing. But he never did get his wish to fight the 'puppet' soldiers in South Vietnam. The fortunes of war brought him instead to this spot beside the Mekong in Cambodia, a foreign country, where he was cut down and his body burned, a thousand miles from home.

The Khmer Rouge were still very much an enigma, a mysterious, invisible force. We did not see much sign of them in the early months of the war. The dead on the battlefields were almost entirely Vietnamese communists, either North Vietnamese or Viet Cong. Then, little by little, that began to change as Vietnamese priorities shifted back to the struggle in South Vietnam and they left the fighting in Cambodia to their creation, the Khmer Rouge.

The bodies in black pyjamas began to be those of dark and swarthy peasant boys from Kompong Thom, Kratie, Stung Treng, all Cambodian provinces which had been captured early in the war and where a ferocious Khmer Rouge recruiting drive and collectivis-ation programme was underway. What had begun in 1970 as a war of 'national resistance' by Lon Nol's supporters to rid Cambodia of

42

50,000 NVA and Viet Cong soldiers was developing into a full-blown civil war.

In Phnom Penh, there was one westerner with unique personal experience of the Khmer Rouge. François Bizot, a man of intransigent sincerity, had come to Cambodia in 1965. He worked with Bernard Groslier, the famous French archaeologist, in the Conservation d'Angkor. Later he became an ethnologist and with extraordinary diligence taught himself to read and write the Cambodian language. His passion was Cambodian Buddhist texts, for which he combed the countryside, riding into distant villages on his BMW motor bike. Bizot was more than a dry academic obsessed with obscure Khmer texts inscribed on palm leaves in ancient Pali script; he was a strong-minded man with an enviable serenity and calm strength. He struggled to understand the mind and feelings of the Cambodian peasant and achieved this better than anyone I know. Ultimately it was an advantage that helped to save his life.

In 1968 his daughter, Hélène, was born in Srah Srang, a village in the shadow of the Bayon temple near Siem Reap. Her mother was a Cambodian girl, under twenty years old. It was a traditional Khmer birth with the birth fire to ward off spirits and the umbilical cord cut with a bamboo stick heated in the flames. In 1970, with the occupation of the temples by the North Vietnamese army, and stray shells falling on the village, Bizot had to abandon Siem Reap and move his family to Phnom Penh for greater safety. They settled into the wooden house next door to Madame Chum's *fumerie*.

One day in October 1971, Bizot went to Oudong, the former capital of the Cambodian kings, twenty miles north of Phnom Penh. He wanted to talk to some monks about some texts. As usual, he took Hélène with him in the Land Rover, but for the last stretch of the journey he left her with her nanny for safekeeping and walked with a guide through the fields to the village.

He was suddenly surrounded by Khmer Rouge soldiers. His hands were tied behind his back and he was led off into the forest, blindfolded. At a Khmer Rouge encampment, he was questioned and accused of being a spy. His interrogator was Kang Kek Ieu, alias Comrade Deuch, the notorious commander-in-chief of the Tuol Sleng prison camp after the Khmer Rouge victory. (Bizot is the only westerner to have set eyes on this torturer and survived.) He was kept tied up and was often blindfolded. It was a terrifying experience in every way, but made more unbearable because he did not know what had happened to his little daughter. (Hélène had been taken back to Phnom Penh by her nanny and was in safe hands.)

In the camp, Bizot befriended a beautiful little girl of about Hélène's age – nearly four. After a few days, her father, a captive Lon Nol soldier, was marched into the forest by the guards and never seen again. Bizot grew fond of this girl, now doubtless an orphan, for he was haunted by the loss of Hélène and saw his daughter in the child. Sometimes they were able to play together. It was an important relationship which he built up to sustain him and to maintain his equilibrium.

But the little girl was forced to attend Khmer Rouge indoctrination classes in the camp. Slowly her attitude towards the tied-up Frenchman changed from one of innocent childish affection to one of doubt and mistrust. Bizot's spirits fell; he could feel her slipping away from him a little more each day. She lost her impish smile, was moody and sullen. Soon the Khmer Rouge possessed complete power over her little mind and she became another child of the revolution, spoon-fed on hate.

The sad climax came a little later. One evening she entered his hut. As usual he was lying, his feet bound together, on the floor. She bent down and coldly and determinedly tried to insert her tiny finger between his ankle and the rope binding. All the time her eyes never left his torn face. When she found she could insert a finger in the gap, she screamed to a Khmer Rouge guard to come and tighten the ropes for they were too loose. This became a spiteful nightly ritual. Bizot found himself at the mercy of the little girl he had befriended, whom the Khmer Rouge had turned into a demon. It was the end of innocence, of a child's love, of Cambodian beauty for him. By the time he was released three months later, the girl was well on her way to becoming another young Khmer Rouge revolutionary. And when Bizot told me the story much later, I understood better the unthinking ease with which very young Khmer Rouge soldiers could execute people without mercy and often for no reason. Order them to shoot their mothers and after such indoctrination they would not hesitate, I thought.

The weeks passed and the Hôtel Le Royal had been renamed Le Phnom, conforming with Cambodia's new status as a republic. It was just as sociable and homely. Beyond its walls, however, the indolent charm of pre-war Cambodia was fading as the city began filling with refugees. The jasmine-sellers were no longer small girls but mutilated soldiers who sidled out of the darkness, crab-like, on crutches. An irreversible process of destruction of a gracious way of life was underway.

One night, I found myself abused and physically attacked in a restaurant by a French planter, angry because I had reported that the communists had established bases in the French-owned rubber plantation at Chamcar Andong. 'Voyou! Perfide Albion!' he cried, yanking my long hair and accusing me of deliberate distortion of the facts and disloyalty to France. The story was quite without merit and would never have been noticed had it not been reprinted in the Phnom Penh press. But the planter was convinced that American reaction would be a B52 air raid on his plantation, resulting in its obliteration. As if the Americans did not have enough of their own intelligence sources to tell them what was going on. His unprovoked attack was symptomatic of the souring of mood.

One day, the door of Studio Six opened and a man and a woman walked in. He was alert, tanned, taut, like a French para, as indeed he had been in Algeria. His name was Jacques Tonnerre and he was now a freelance French photographer. His companion was called Jacqueline. Her father was French and her mother Vietnamese and she lived with her mother in a little house in Saigon. She had been Claude Arpin's girlfriend and she was here on a sad mission, to collect his belongings to return them to his family in France. As she bent to pick up the rucksack and camera bag off the floor, there was an expression of unbearable pain in her eyes.

We exchanged a few words and I said I was bitterly sorry. Then she was gone, back to Saigon. I watched her leave the studio but, forced suddenly into silence before her sadness and beauty, I never even said *au revoir*. In that instant, however, I felt a silent complicity and regretted our casual parting. She was suffering dreadfully.

Soon after this the Cambodian authorities revoked my journalist's visa. I never found out why, but can only assume that it was because of my story about the communist occupation of the French rubber plantations. I had no choice but to leave the city to which I had begun to form such a strong emotional attachment. There was a possibility that I would be recalled to Paris, bringing a curtain down on my Indo-China adventure before it had really begun, and the following days were an agony of fretting. In the end, my French bosses at AFP came to the rescue. They asked me to get a South Vietnamese visa and become AFP's envoyé special in Saigon.

Jacqueline

I feel good that
at least now I have a place
to begin to settle down
and simply wait for the start
of a routine
and the rapid passing of time
and the days and the weeks
that it will all
spill into . . .

There are some cities that burn into our consciousness the moment we arrive. Saigon in 1970 was such a place. It was only a hundred miles distant, but a whole world away from the capital of Cambodia. The massive US involvement made it the middle of the world. From Phnom Penh, the airplane rose quickly above the clouds, too high to make out the ground; but, as it descended, less than an hour later, the suffering landscape of South Vietnam was piteously visible. Bomb craters littered the green rice fields and clustered like a terrible pox around the waterways; here and there, the earth was torn out to accommodate giant military bases.

Then the Air Vietnam jet hit turbulence and was tossed up and down like a yo-yo. I later found that planes almost always did so in the final stages of their approach to Saigon; as if the airspace around the wartime capital of South Vietnam were controlled by a malevolent genie.

Suddenly we were through the fortress of clouds. I saw the grey elbow of the Saigon river along which the city spreads, watchtowers, buildings, hangars, supply depots, a church; and we were skimming along the runway of the busiest airport in the world, taxiing past row upon row of fat-bellied troop-carriers, helicopters, fighter-bombers, all the glittering, hi-tech machinery that made the Vietnam war.

I stepped onto the hot tarmac of Tan Son Nhut air base to the ear-splitting howl of jet fighters. These jets had an aura of aggression, with their pointed noses painted as sharks hurtling down the runway, bombs tucked under wings, afterburners aglow. The energy of the war was awesome. As time went by, it would become infectious, even obsessive. I did not realise then, as I collected my bags and headed into town, tired and crumpled by the journey and the baking heat, that this was to be my home for much of the next four years. Welcome to the Republic of Vietnam.

Saigon, the once languid Paris of the Orient, was a frenzied place by comparison with the Phnom Penh I had left behind. Americans were everywhere. The streets stank of exhaust fumes, choked by an endless torrent of motor bikes, army lorries, cars, jeeps, cyclos, buses, American embassy cars and little blue-and-yellow Renault taxis like Noddy cars, a throwback to pre-war times. Its pavements round the old French opera house, the centrepiece of the city, were crowded with girls in *aó dàis*, street-hawkers, beggars, orphans. Amid the din of traffic and the raucous blare of juke-boxes rose the whining plaintive cry of the beggar children: 'Hey you, Jo. You Number One. You gimme money.' It was clear that the price of American intervention was terrible; not just in terms of human lives, but also on Vietnamese culture and the fabric of Vietnamese society.

At noon, the mood changed, the cacophony ceased. The steel shutters clanged down. The shops closed. It was the hour of *le déjeuner* followed by *la sieste*. The streets slumbered in sunstruck silence until three o'clock, when the clamour resumed. For a short while, the magic charm of old Saigon reasserted itself.

I slipped into a restaurant and asked for a table. 'Avec plaisir, Monsieur,' said the old waiter. The cultural collision between America and the old Vietnam of French days never ceased to bewilder and fascinate me. I knew which I preferred. I ached to see a white képi bobbing down the street instead of an American baseball cap, to hear Edith Piaf and Juliette Greco instead of Baby Huey and the Mamas and the Papas.

I was not involved in as much ground combat with the Grunts – American ground troops – as with the South Vietnamese army (ARVN). By now, President Nixon's programme of de-Americanising or Vietnamising the war was well advanced; US combat troops were being phased out of battle. There were still tens of thousands of support troops, but with anti-war feeling building in the US orders were to keep US casualties to a minimum. Also, I liked to be with the ARVN. I could never forget that Vietnam was their country, and that this was their war, and I developed a terrific admiration for some of their units – the Airborne; the First Infantry Division; the Marines, whose soldiers at the front invariably made me welcome and shared their food. On the other hand, I spent a lot of time riding on US choppers – ferried in and out of firebases and landing zones, both hot and cold, by the First Air Cavalry (Airmobile) – until sitting on the cramped and juddering floor of an open-sided Huey carrying heavily armed GIs on operations became second nature. As a result, there are few more emotive sights in the world for me than a line of Hueys on a mission silhouetted against the stunted trees and the sky, and no more emotive sound than the rhythmic 'whap-whap' of their rotor blades beating the air. Even today, the sound gives me the shivers.

The choppers were the workhorses of the US army and their crews among the heroes of the war. They flew in almost all weather, every day, in and out of battle zones, without question, without drama. The drill was to hurry out to the helicopter pad early in the morning, to hitch whatever rides were going. The pilot and co-pilot sat in the nose of the 'bird' and a door-gunner sat on each side, armed with an M60 machine gun.

The GIs, counting days until they went home, could never understand why British reporters were in Vietnam, let alone wanted to be there. 'Goddamn, you volunteered to be in 'Nam,' they said. 'You must be a crazy son of a bitch.'

There was little time to get acquainted with Saigon, to discover its ways and secret places, its underlying anguish; or, indeed, to recall Cambodia. In early 1971, the Pentagon decided to launch a ground assault on the Ho Chi Minh trail, in which ARVN troops with US logistical, artillery and air-support would cut the North Vietnamese supply lines by capturing the strategically important trail-town of Tchepone inside eastern Laos. Codenamed Lam Son 719, it was the biggest airmobile operation in history; and it ended in disaster, despite the massive US support.

Days beforehand, long columns of US military transport, deuce-and-a-half trucks, M60 tanks, armoured cars and men, all poured one way, to the border with Laos where the North Vietnamese army lay among the hills, waiting for the assault. Ambushes were common on QL9, the Yellow Brick Road linking Quang Tri, the rear logistics base, with the forward combat base at Khe Sanh reactivated specially for the occasion. The American armoured convoys drove along it at speed, whirling huge dust clouds behind. The dust-choked soldiers, eyes covered by sand-goggles, fingered 'peace' signs in the air.

Standing on a low hill overlooking Khe Sanh one day, I saw scores of helicopters lined up – Hueys, twin-rotored Chinooks, Cobra gunships. Then the rockets came in with a whoosh and the helicopters were 'scrambled', swarming into the sky like locusts. A French reporter, who had been a paratroop captain at the siege of Dien Bien Phu, shook his head in amazement at this display of American strength. 'If only . . .' he said. In 1954, at the time of Dien Bien Phu, the French Corps Expéditionnaire in Indo-China had but four helicopters to its name.

Tragedy struck once again; in a sudden but not totally unexpected way. Larry Burrows, perhaps the most brilliant war photographer of his generation and a man with a gentle and chivalrous nature; Kent Potter, my opium-smoking companion from Cambodia; Henri Huet, a gifted French photographer; and Keisaburo Shimamota of Japan, together with several senior South Vietnamese officers, were shot down on a reconnaissance mission over Laos. The leading helicopter, carrying the officers, was hit by anti-aircraft fire. Instead of turning away in a safe circle, the pilot of the second helicopter continued on the same course into a hail of 50-calibre machine-gun fire and was shot down with all the photographers on board. The helicopter was seen to be hit, to burst into flames, crash, explode and burn. That evening the mood in the press hut was sombre.

The Pentagon had explicitly prohibited journalists from flying in

and out of Laos as passengers aboard US helicopters; justifying the
ban by citing a law forbidding the US military from flying civilians
across an international boundary without that country's permission.
In reality, it was to maintain the fiction that Lam Son 719 was an
all-ARVN operation, with the Americans providing just logistics and
air support, the Pentagon being anxious to prove that 'Vietnamis-
ation' of the war was successful. So the photographers' deaths were
blamed, by the American press in particular, on the poor quality of
the ARVN helicopter pilots. At that night's press briefing, Colonel
Hien, the chief South Vietnamese spokesman, was subjected to a
barrage of abuse and insults. It was not his fault. He was as saddened
as anyone and did not deserve the tongue-lashing.

Knowing the dead photographers, I felt they would not have
reproached the South Vietnamese. A photographer in wartime knows
that his job might entail the sacrifice of his life. He knows the perils
of death just as closely as a soldier; and in Vietnam, without question,
a photographer faced danger far more often than the average US
soldier. The majority of the half-a-million GIs serving in Vietnam
at the peak of the American presence were supply soldiers or clerks,
REMFs – Rear-Echelon Mother-Fuckers – in the jargon of the
combat troops. Larry, Kent, Henri and Shimamota were not
demoralised by the dangers inherent in their profession – far from
it – and were prepared to take their chances with the South Vietnamese in the field. None of them would willingly give up a seat in a
helicopter; they were too absorbed in photographing the war to feel
afraid.

Nonetheless, their deaths were incredibly sad and the ugly aftermath left a bitter taste. I think even the hardest-bitten of us could
not keep aloof from it. I remember sitting disconsolately on my

bunk wondering who among us would be next. In Vietnam, when American GIs lost best buddies they used to say, 'it don't mean nothin', by which they meant, of course, it meant everything. We said the same that night, for our dead friends meant the world to us.

In the aftermath of the crash, having verified there were no survivors, the Americans put an airstrike directly on the spot where the helicopters went down, to prevent secret military documents falling into enemy hands. Searches after the war have found no trace of wreckage or of our photographer friends whose graves are now the jungle.

American pilots also made potentially lethal errors, of course, as I found when I flew on the last US helicopter back to Quang Tri combat base one evening. Rising from the runway out of Khe Sanh, it picked up ground fire. Then, flying a course down QL9, the winding dirt road which snakes round the mountains and past the infamous Rock Pile, a jagged hill the site of many ambushes, the pilot became lost in the gathering gloom. The first I knew was when he thwacked the helicopter down hard in a field, borrowed my Zippo lighter and studied his map. The door gunners gripped their M60 machine guns and stared intently into the inky darkness. Our ears strained for sound; we were in hostile territory; every second on the ground felt too long.

Airborne again, I felt at once a weird sensation stab my stomach. The pilot was suffering from vertigo; he had lost his bearings. The controls were no longer solid in his hands; the helicopter was thrashing about in the sky, yawing, beginning to slip out of control. It could only be a matter of seconds before we crashed or were shot down. The machine lurched, then dropped towards the earth. I was sitting next to the open door looking down, sensing the ground coming up to meet me, my fingers digging into the seat, my body tensing for the crash. But at the last moment a searchlight caught us in its beam, the pilot regained control and we were guided down to Cam Lo, the most northerly firebase in South Vietnam, seconds from disaster for we were about to crash or fly across the border into North Vietnam. After this experience, I did not really mind whose helicopter I travelled in – South Vietnamese or American.

It was easy to disparage and make jokes about the Americans. Few had any concept of the values of the country in which they fought. They denigrated the Vietnamese as yellow 'gooks'. But their energy was inexhaustible. In those days, the atmosphere in the warrant-officers' club of the Air Cavalry at Quang Tri combat base was often moving and emotional.

The helicopters, flying hundreds of sorties daily in and out of Laos, had shown an acute vulnerability to the heavy anti-aircraft fire put up by the NVA. They were being tested, for the first time, in what amounted to the lethal environment of a 'medium intensity' war. The US army was losing scores of them, so many that it was running out of trained helicopter pilots to keep the machines in the air. But the generals saw Lam Son 719 as a rehearsal for a future war in Europe against the Soviet Red Army; the pilots and their machines were expendable.

Every week brought a fresh batch of clean and innocent-faced young men to Quang Tri, replacements scarcely out of flying school in the US. There was an initiation rite before they joined their unit. The newcomers were put on stage in the warrant-officers' club. The air was loud with shouts and singing of 'You're Going Home in a Body Bag' to the tune 'Camptown Races'. They were then bombarded with beer and Coke cans and debagged. Sure enough, the day after the celebrations one or two of them were indeed shipped home in plastic body bags when the helicopters they were piloting disappeared over the mountains of Laos.

It was the unusual and moving custom to turn the names of the dead and missing in action upside down on a roll of honour fixed to the wall. Each evening when we returned from the field, we looked at the list with a shiver of recognition. I asked a passing pilot how he felt. He said he could not understand why so many of his buddies were dying in Laos when officially the US was not at war there. Neither could I. At such times, Quang Tri emitted all the daredevil atmosphere, good comradeship and sense of duty of a fighter-pilot squadron during the Battle of Britain. It was at those times that I came to realise how cruel this war was for the young men of America.

> If you are able,
> save for them a place
> inside of you
> and save one backward glance
> when you are leaving
> for the places they can
> no longer go.
> Be not ashamed to say
> you loved them,
> though you may
> or may not have always.
> Take what they have left
> and what they have taught you

with their dying
and keep it with your own.
And in that time
when men decide and feel safe
to call the war insane,
take one moment to embrace
those gentle heroes
you left behind.

One morning, a helicopter dropped three of us on a section of the Ho Chi Minh trail captured by South Vietnamese parachutists. The track was narrow and winding, camouflaged for about a kilometre by a lattice of creepers and vines. Patches of harsh sunlight broke through in narrow beams. But for the most part we were cloaked in darkness – an eerie feeling. It was as if we were travelling through an underground tunnel.

Finally, we clambered up a hill, into the open. Very high up, a formation of B52 bombers flew from the east, threads of vapour trailing from all eight engines. Across the valley, clouds of dust rose hundreds of feet, blotting out the sky; the ground trembled, and the landscape was filled with rolling thunder. The B52 raids made Laos the most bombed nation in history; 2,093,100 tons of bombs, more than were dropped on Nazi Germany. I thought of the pilots and aircrews heading back to Guam who would never see the consequences of their raids and I wondered about their feelings.

After a month, the South Vietnamese forces were cruelly routed, despite the massive US air cover. Of the 17,000 strong invasion force, 5000 were killed or wounded. Nearly 200 Americans died. The South Vietnamese pulled out in panic, sometimes hanging on, in desperation and haste, to the helicopter skids. Inevitably their grip weakened, they slipped and plunged to their deaths in the hills below. Hundreds of dead were left behind, as well as machinery and equipment.

This mountain of war debris is still there, decaying slowly in the clammy jungle heat, the flotsam and jetsam of a tragically misconceived campaign to cut the Ho Chi Minh trail and seize North Vietnam's own heavily defended backyard.

Sometimes a group of us would cadge a lift in a US Marine Corps helicopter to Da Nang, headquarters of the 1st Marine Division, for a day's relaxation. We stayed in Da Nang press club, next to the famous museum of Cham art, ate T-bone steaks, watched a movie, drank, spent an hour or two being pleasured at the Pink House, looked out for a pretty woman on China Beach, rolled in the surf. Once, we watched a USO show for officers. Korean go-go dancers in little purple panties gyrated in front of an all-male audience. Suddenly there was pandemonium; shouts, screams, a battle for the exits, acrid smoke. A couple of CS gas grenades had burst among us. The culprit was an angry GI, bitter at his exclusion from the party. Next time, he said, it would be a fragmentation grenade. The military police were not amused.

The paradox of Vietnam was that there was not another country on earth under the shadow of such misery. Most American soldiers found it the most wretched experience of their lives, and for the Vietnamese the suffering was terrible, a tyrant from which there was no escape. The huge American military effort was prolonging the war. Yet the war provided a magnificent arena for adventure. The truth of Michael Herr's remark in *Dispatches* that Vietnam was what we had 'instead of happy childhoods' was, for me, exact. Those deadly but exhilarating toys of war – the helicopters, the gunships, the jet fighters – gripped our imagination. We could experience them all. Great swathes of Vietnam were free fire zones where the Americans killed anything that moved. But Vietnam was an adventure playground for journalism, a place for a young man to test and be tested in the most exotic environment imaginable. The proximity of death amid such beauty seemed to give, to me at least, a quality to life unattainable elsewhere.

Everything seemed possible and our existence had many strange moments. By night, we journalists could join a C119 gunship, 'zapping' supply trucks coming down the Ho Chi Minh trail, watching in awe as the Gatling-style machine guns mounted in its belly spewed out 6000 rounds a minute into the jungle below; by day we could be swimming in the surf in the immense dazzling blue of the South China Sea. We could equally be on the ground, sloshing up to the armpits through oozing mud in the Mekong Delta or belly-crawling for cover amid a mortar attack on a firebase below the demilitarised zone (DMZ) between North and South Vietnam. The war continued every day as if part of sunlight itself from the Delta to the DMZ, but each experience was different, and reporting it was always strenuous, gruelling and emotionally draining, but unforgettable nevertheless. At the beginning, I was so mesmerised by the war that I felt a spasm of regret when President Nixon announced a major withdrawal of American forces, fearing it would end just as I had come on the scene.

*

JACQUELINE

At the end of March, I returned to Saigon. To come back to it from the field, utterly worn out and filthy, hair and sweat-soaked fatigues encrusted in red laterite dust from the Khe Sanh plateau, helicopter rotor blades still reverberating in my ears, but with the exhilaration of being alive, was a powerful experience. The city blazed with all the passion, intrigue and insanity of a wartime capital.

After several weeks away, the first rule was to drink a symbolic *apéritif* on the terrace of the Continental Palace, Saigon's great colonial hotel owned by Philippe Francini, scion of one of Saigon's oldest métis families and famous for his erotic paintings. It was impossible not to like the Continental, with its green shutters, gently rotating ceiling fans, its shabby, romantic air and its staff who always seemed to be sleeping on mats in the long corridors. We basked in the fantasy that Graham Greene had written *The Quiet American* there.

In the middle of the hotel was a small garden. Nothing was so far from the clamour of the choking, fume-ridden streets outside – the lights, the bars, the rock music, the women – than the harmony and warm stillness of this secret garden. I sometimes went there for a late evening drink amid the frangipani and hibiscus blossom, the fairy lights and consoling singing of cicadas. It was the reverse of the frenzy of war, and a good place to think.

The older waiters in their starched white uniforms, bobbing back and forth from the bar with ice and soda, had been working at the hotel since French colonial days, as had its rotund, immaculately dressed manager, Monsieur Loi. There was always a boisterous crowd on the terrace outside: US officers making small talk with their girls, whose Asian faces and petite figures contrasted with the clumsy bulk of these beer-bellied Americans; children whining for money; groups of journalists whose usual means of relaxation were the same as any returned soldier from the front – alcohol, women and food. The journalists congregated at the little round tables in rattan armchairs and recounted again and again their favourite stories of war and sex.

There was a well-worn routine that went like this; first, off to one of Saigon's Corsican-run restaurants near the flower market for a French meal washed down with wine; then to Mimi's, or some other girlie bar, for more drinks and entertainment. Midnight and curfew was the hour of decision. The urgent need for a woman meant all sorts of compromises were made.

Amid the blood, mud and heartbreak of the battlefields, we all dreamt of savouring one delicious sensation: the moment when we would wake up, in safety, in Saigon, between clean sheets, with an exotic Vietnamese woman in our arms. Sometimes we were lucky and savoured a thrill utterly beyond the reach of our normal, daily, deadly world of war in the rice fields. Then, only then, did we know that we were truly alive, and perhaps the sensation gave some of us a glimpse into what Kipling meant when he wrote 'Eastern beds are softer'. But there were other nights which ended in trouble, sordidness, sexual emptiness, disgust or regret; screwing mechanically in some sleazy hotel catering for raunchy GIs and their whores.

> I became a student
> of Nha Trang today
> a city by the sea.
> I approached it as a child
> for I am still a virgin
> of the war.

It's full of Catholic priests
and allied soldiers
and Buddhist priests
and other soldiers
and garbage
that seems to belong
exactly where it is . . .
I can't say I learned a thing
and I couldn't find a whore,
though I'm sure there are more than
a few . . .
I couldn't find a need . . .

This time, I came back to Saigon with a vague premonition that my life was about to change. A few days later it did. A chance midday appointment took me to the old Rex Hotel, headquarters of JUSPAO, or Joint United States Public Affairs Office, the American propaganda machine in Vietnam which looked after the huge Saigon press corps and where the 'Five o'clock Follies', the daily press briefings, used to be held. There, amid the scented flowers of Nguyên Huế Street, I met Jacqueline again.

No day, I thought, could have been brighter. Other memories of Saigon have been dimmed by the forgetfulness of time; the magic of that encounter has still not faded from my recollection. Her unconscious grace, her gentle, faintly Vietnamese eyes, her smile, the appealing curve of her nutbrown body remain so vivid. She stood in a simple flowered dress in the noonday sun, untouched, and to me untamed and unattainable, a true child of nature.

I completely missed my JUSPAO appointment. We took a dented yellow-and-blue Renault taxi to the French colonial sports club, the

Cercle Sportif, for lunch and a swim with her friends. As the cab rattled up rue Pasteur, past the AFP office, past Doc Lap presidential palace, along a wide avenue bordered with trees, I was totally absorbed in her and the exotic blend of Franco-Vietnamese culture she represented. I realised with a jolt, that my intuition had been right. I had a strong feeling when we had first met in Phnom Penh that I would fall in love with her if I ever saw her again.

It seems unjust now to bring Jacqueline into this story, for the roots we put down in Saigon have since been torn up and may never grow back again. But I cannot look back to those formative Indo-China years without allusion to her. At first, the loss of Claude, the first man she loved, lay across our relationship like a physical barrier. She had loved him without compromise. She was petrified of an emotional entanglement with another journalist, a species she saw, through eyes shadowed by the tragedy of his disappearance, as harbingers of uncertainty and unhappiness. Nor did she want to be a prey to one of Saigon's petty love affairs.

She was on the defensive, and I did not dare to insist. When, finally, we acknowledged our love, it was outside Indo-China, in Malaysia, on a holiday snatched a few months later; exploring Penang, swimming at the Lone Pine beach hotel, exploring the Cameron Highlands, sleeping where we stopped, touching hands amid the soothing cadence of a tropical night. It was an entrancing setting that inspired fantastic dreams; soon she became the person I loved most in all the world.

It was a love that sustained me for the rest of my time in Indo-China, enabling me to escape from the horrors of the war into something truly romantic. Not only was she wildly beautiful – considered by many to be the beauty of Saigon – but she was also unceasingly loyal and when I stumbled in life she was there to pick me up again.

Jacqueline lived in a narrow side street near the end of Tu Do, formerly Catinat, the main thoroughfare of Saigon which runs down from the pink basilica to the Saigon river. She was in charge of the Saigon office of the *Overseas Weekly*, a hard-biting alternative paper for GIs in Vietnam that told the war as it really was. The generals banned it from sale in the PX, but it still sold well. Her mother, Regine, was a dressmaker, a saintly woman who had known more than life's share of unhappiness, and who was deeply involved with the local Red Cross Association and the blood bank at the Hôpital Grall, the old French military hospital. Her father, who had first arrived in Indo-China on a Messageries Maritimes boat from Marseilles, was living again in France. Jacqueline was a product of Saigon's famous convent, the Couvent des Oiseaux. As well as French and Vietnamese, she spoke faultless English, learnt from the convent's English teacher, a fierce little Scot. She enthralled me once by reciting a passage of Robert Burns's poetry. *Le Petit Prince* by Antoine de Saint-Exupéry was the book that she really loved.

She had never known Vietnam without war. It was there when she was born; it was there as she grew up. For all she knew, it would be there when she died. She belonged to a fated generation. Yet she could not conceive of life anywhere else. She personified freedom, straining to hang on to a life which seemed to have been more and more Utopian as the war dragged on.

There was nothing more enchanting than the sun playing on her face, lighting eyes full of expression and appeal. The simplest pleasures – a bowl of noodles in the street, dancing, going to the cinema, swimming at the Cercle Sportif, talking – took on a new allure: and when the war permitted it, she showed me *her* Vietnam. We travelled to Hué, the former imperial capital and the spiritual centre of Vietnam; to the cool hills and pine forests of Dalat; and, on quiet Sundays, to Vung Tau near the mouths of the Mekong, the sea-resort closest to Saigon which the French called Cap Saint-Jacques.

Such journeys were light-years from those I was making when covering the war. Jacqueline, by her very presence, brought the Vietnamese landscape alive for me. The inescapableness of death, which I had so often felt, faded into the background, replaced by the joy of living. I saw the Vietnamese countryside in a new light.

This freshness of vision was particularly strong on the afternoon we took a small sampan from Hué up the River of Perfumes. Fugitives for a few hours during an uneasy lull in the war, we were making a pilgrimage to one of the emperors' tombs lost in the eastern foothills of the Annam mountain range. Behind us, we had left a city infected by violence.

The North Vietnamese army had crossed the demarcation line along the 17th parallel and fought their way to within a few miles of Hué's northern gates. A swollen multitude of refugees were streaming southward out of the city, fearing a repeat of Tet 1968. The mood in Hué was suddenly sinister and dangerous. Retreating, demoralised, drunken ARVN soldiers had looted and burned down the market; shells screamed intermittently overhead, to crash into houses around the citadel.

We were only a few miles away, gliding up the river through a beautiful valley of green-carpeted rice fields rimmed by distant peaks. We were lapped by warmth. When we arrived, we sat for a while, lulled by the ageless serenity of the tomb. It was a world of quiet and spirituality, the silence so complete that we felt we were in the presence of the infinite. Later, as we glided downriver at sunset, the water shimmered like bronze in the sun; farmers drove their buffalo home through darkening fields; and, as the shadows lengthened and the gaunt mountains turned blue, we quite forgot the war.

No other city is so representative of Vietnamese culture and learning as Hué, seat of the former emperors of Annam; and no other city has such a tragic recent history. In 1968 it was devastated by the Tet offensive. The Viet Cong seized the red-walled citadel and much of the city around it. For a month, the blue, red and yellow flag of the Viet Cong's National Liberation Front fluttered defiantly over the ramparts of the citadel, symbol of Vietnamese nationhood.

The US Marine Corps, supported by airpower, retaliated; devastating large populated parts of Hué. Using terrifying firepower, phosphorus and napalm bombs, they blitzed the Viet Cong from the citadel. Some of the ornate temples, throne rooms and altars where the Annamite princes had received their mandate from heaven right up to the beginning of World War Two – many years after such Confucian rites had been abolished by Peking itself – were turned into rubble. This caused deep-seated resentment against the Americans.

The heroism of the Viet Cong was phenomenal. They said they were fighting for liberty and were prepared to die for it. Many ordinary people in Hué, disgusted by the degradation of the war, its filth and corruption, admired their disciplined purity and nationalism even though they did not want the communists in power.

The discovery after this withdrawal of the hastily-buried remains of thousands of Hué officials and their families in mass graves, massacred out of vengeance, tarnished for ever this vision of Viet Cong patriotism. Neither side in the Vietnam war behaved well, as we know too well from the barbarism of the plump Lieutenant Calley and his hate-filled men at My Lai. The Hué massacre by the Viet Cong ranks with My Lai among the most disgusting atrocities of the war.

Small wonder that Hué, weighed down by that terrible baggage, exuded an underlying melancholy. It is a garden city of parks, shady streets, palm-fringed villas, a school where Ho Chi Minh and other revolutionaries were educated, a university. Amid the dark despair of war, it was the River of Perfumes cutting through its centre that gave it that special, magic quality. Some evenings, just to be on the water, we hired a sampan instead of staying in the overcrowded journalists' hotel with its tribe of king-size rats and permanent undercurrent of nervous tension, and where it was all too easy to feel trapped, as in a prison.

As curfew fell at 9p.m., we were poled out to the middle of the river where we anchored with a huddle of other sampans, visible in the darkness only by their winking lights. The hills around glowed red with fighting, but we slept snugly in a little matted cabin, knowing that the river was the safest place to be. Periodically, cockle-shell barques crept out of the inky blackness, bearing steaming bowls of *phò*, the Vietnamese soup, and ripe mounds of tropical fruits. It was in Hué that Jacqueline introduced me to the *Tale of Kieu*, Vietnam's romantic literary classic, an extended narrative love poem about a young girl of the Mandarin class who is forced to submit to every humiliation but who emerges true to herself.

Without knowing something of Kieu, it is impossible to appreciate

70

the dignity, passion and melancholia which reside in Vietnamese women. The beautiful, strong-willed Kieu is representative of Vietnam, overcome but not conquered, not servile but a survivor.

Those nights on the sampan were some of the most perfect I spent in Indo-China. The bombing lit up the night sky. But our eyelids were shut against the red flash of these false dawns. Only in the morning, with the long overhead shriek and searing crunch of the first salvo impacting on Hué's northern bank, did we wake, pole ourselves to the steps of the Huong Giang Hotel and begin the day afresh.

Inevitably at such times, a few of us went in search of the one place in Hué where it was possible to smoke opium. It was a small house near the citadel behind a flyblown Chinese restaurant, the only eating house still functioning in Hué. A broken-toothed, shrivelled old man with a goatee beard, himself an opium addict, lived there with his grown children. While he prepared our pipes, the old rascal told us how, masquerading as a hairdresser, he had spied on the French army during the French Indo-China war. He had provided the Viet Minh with scraps of intelligence gleaned while cutting the French officers' hair. Our arrival was fortuitous; our dollars enabled him to build a magnificent bunker fortified with sandbags to shelter in with his family during the shelling; the next time we went he invited us to smoke inside it, and we felt supremely safe. Hué was the only place in Vietnam where I felt it appropriate to smoke opium – it suited the softness of the imperial city's mood as it had Phnom Penh.

North of Hué, for thirty miles up to the demilitarised zone, stretched the narrow, sandy, grey and drizzly coastal plain between the Annamite mountains and the blue waters of the South China Sea. The French army had lugubriously named it La Rue Sans Joie. Here, some of the most bloody struggles of the Vietnam war were fought at Quang Tri, Dong Ha, Cam Lo, the US Marine Corps firebase at Con Thien, still with rusting relics of its past as a Foreign Legion outpost. It is an area scarred by death, confusion, fear and heroism. The blood of men from many nations has soaked into its sandy soil.

I got to know this grim area intimately, and especially during the eight-month battle for Quang Tri in the Easter 1972 communist offensive. I remember it now with nostalgia and a glint of terror. Sights and sounds spin through my head: patrols melting into the wilderness of misty rain like phantoms from the underworld; the belch of mortar rounds socking into the mud; straggly lines of refugees trudging down Highway One; dogs tearing at bodies; the constant rumble of artillery; brave smiles; helicopters against a darkening sky; the subdued moan of the wounded in the night; bullets everywhere.

Who remembers it now?

One of the reasons I do is because of Gérard Hubert, a freelance photographer. He had drifted into Saigon claiming to be a French Canadian and soon established a reputation for courage. He had an almost mythical rapport with the Vietnamese Airborne, the élite of the South Vietnamese army, and showed mysterious soldierly qualities. Once, his helicopter was shot down and another time he dragged three Airborne soldiers to safety under heavy fire. He was cited for bravery. On yet another occasion he was wounded, but with a true soldier's conception of duty insisted on handing in his film before he sought hospital treatment for a nasty shrapnel wound in the shoulder. Hubert was a delightfully unassuming, uncommunicative man, especially on matters concerning his past. I saw him one day amid heavy fighting on the edge of Quang Tri. The next day he was dead, decapitated by a 130mm shell which scored a direct hit on the command post.

When the Canadians said they knew nothing about Hubert, the mystery deepened. Inquiries revealed that he had been in prison, hence his reticence. It was also discovered that he had been a French paratrooper in Algeria – hence his love of, and identification with, the Vietnamese Airborne, an offspring of the French paras. Quite rightly, he was buried with full military honours in the French cemetery in Saigon, a lost, angry but courageous man who sought and seemed to find fulfilment in the lunacy of the Vietnam war.

Two years later I made a bizarre visit to the Street Without Joy; it left a bitterly sad impression. The area was one of the most devastated parts of South Vietnam, but briefly, after the 1973 ceasefire, something like peace prevailed and it became part of a battlefield package tour. Air Vietnam, keen to promote tourism, was flying in tourists on weekend trips from Saigon for US$80. 'Visit the historic battlefields of Quang Tri,' its brochure said. 'See with your own eyes how much Vietnam has suffered through more than twenty-five years of war and yet still survived.'

Every building of any size was flattened – mainly by bombing from B52s and Phantom jets and shells from the eight-inch guns of American ships offshore. La Vang basilica, one of the most beautiful cathedrals in South Vietnam, was a broken shell with a splintered statue of Christ among the rubble.

The tourist party from Saigon gazed in shock and silence at the broken shell of the cathedral, but after a while other instincts prevailed. Timidly at first, then with undignified abandon, they posed for family snaps in front of its bullet-spattered walls and amid the piles of rubble in its blitzed interior.

Outside, in the sunlight, a gaggle of barefoot urchins, refugee children of the war, stamped their tiny feet up and down and chanted 'You, Numbah One', evidently hoping to cadge a few *piastres*. The visitors moved on to study other ruins.

One of the party was Monsieur Benoit, a Frenchman from Toulouse, who was on a trip down memory lane. In 1953, he had fought near Quang Tri with the French army against the Viet Minh. It was a fact he made sure nobody forgot. Now he was hoping to catch a sight, a sound, or a particular smell that would conjure up his lost youth.

He was a jovial fellow, who harboured an acute dislike for all things American. In spasms of anger, he would accuse the United States of a whole spectrum of crimes, from cutting down the tall trees lining Saigon's boulevards to sabotage of the Anglo-French Concorde project. The destruction of La Vang basilica was the last straw. 'Partout où ils vont, ils sèment de la merde.'

Most of the twenty-five others on the tour were secretaries at the American embassy in Saigon. Bespectacled, middle-aged career women with a conservative outlook and with a deep-rooted belief in the nobility of what America had done in Vietnam, they went to Quang Tri to express their solidarity with the anti-communist struggle. 'We want to see with our own eyes the extent of the damage,' they said. 'The Vietnamese are beautiful people and it saddens us enormously that they aren't allowed to live in peace.'

There was also a chubby American contractor. He proudly told me that he had been stationed in Cu Chi, near Saigon in 1965. 'I've never dared go back,' he said. 'I'm scared stiff I might be recognised. One day, you see, I was shacking up in this house in a village when six gooks walked in. I guessed they were 'Cong and I grabbed my M14, put it on automatic and blew them clean away.'

As the jet glided over central Vietnam, he said, 'Wow! Very beautiful lakes you have there, very blue.' Jacqueline's mother, Regine, who had accompanied me on this strange and disillusioning tour of her battered homeland, turned to him and said: 'Those aren't lakes. Those are B52 bomb craters.' Her voice silenced his boasting.

Dalat was another exit from the war. The solitude and cool bright weather of the old French hill station, 190 miles north of Saigon, was a relief from the hubbub and heavy damp heat of the capital. The magnificent alpine scenery reminded me of another world. Here, during a period of calm, I went with Jacqueline, walked the mountain paths, ate some of the best French food in Asia at the L'Eau Vive, run by an order of giggling, guitar-playing Catholic nuns; and stayed in the ex-Emperor Bao-Dai's palace, now a hotel. So much of Vietnam was in ruins. But in Dalat you would not have known. Standing on my balcony in the half-light, looking across the little lake to the empty hills, I understood more than ever why Jacqueline did not want to leave.

Two hours from Saigon, at the mouth of the Saigon river, was a very different Vietnam – the beach resort of Vung Tau. The GIs went there for in-country rest and recuperation, the Saigonese for weekends. The beach was magnificent, extending for a couple of miles. The closed area reserved for GIs was sealed off with barbed wire. On the drive down, it was not unknown to pass bodies of Viet Cong laid out in lines beside the road like trophies at a big game shoot. They had been shot during the night and were there to serve as a warning to the populace. But once at the beach, surfing through the waves, no one thought any more of guns.

Jacqueline and my job at Agence France-Presse opened up a fascinating and intriguing Franco-Vietnamese milieu, usually closed to most English journalists. I found that there was still a real bond between the French and the Saigonese based on a common education. French influence was especially strong among the older generation, still imbued with French thought, while the young Vietnamese were enthralled by French films; their favourite film stars were Alain Delon and Jean-Paul Belmondo. There were the usual distractions like the Club Nautique where people waterskied on a tributary of the Saigon river, but there was also another 'scene': philosophical discussions as on the Left Bank of Paris, an underlying sense of Marseilles-style decadence which was attractive, and many other possibilities, a sense that in sultry Saigon anything could happen, and it often did. The best of the French resented the intrusion of the Americans. Still, once a fortnight they used to take on the US or Australian army at rugby. They liked their parties, especially the traditional New Year's Eve 'Light at the End of the Tunnel' party, put on with the spooks of the Saigon CIA station.

76

One French figure I got to know well was Monsieur Jean Ottavj, the proprietor of the old Hôtel Royal. A Corsican, he had spent more than thirty years in Saigon. There were more important and more influential French people about – the diplomats, the planters, the businessmen – but there was none who was kinder. For a while, his hotel was home to myself and a few other British journalists. Monsieur Ottavj was an opium addict and his crinkled face was parchment-white. He liked to relate how he had once smoked with Monsieur Graham Greene. 'Un homme très particulier, un vrai gentilhomme,' he used to say. He lived on the premises. In the afternoons the upstairs corridor reeked; the sickly-sweet, unmistakable odour of opium leaking from the gap under his bedroom door.

Ottavj, who was touchingly superstitious, attributed the war to the imminent end of the world. 'Nostradamus a tout prévu,' he used to say to us with his knowing look. In his last years he confused Greene with the fictional newspaperman, Thomas Fowler, hero of his Indo-Chinese novel, *The Quiet American*. 'Monsieur Greene, pourquoi a-t-il tué l'Americain?' he asked us. Ottavj had a special fondness for the English, which started when a Mrs Simpson used to bring a group of demure English ladies up from Singapore to Saigon for *thés dansants* at his hotel in the 1950s.

When he was awarded the Légion d'Honneur, we organised a dinner in his honour. It was attended in an exceptional gesture by Brooks-Richards, the British ambassador at that time and a former member of Special Operations Executive, and continued over calvados until well after curfew.

Then there was Dominique, *patron* of the Valinco restaurant. After a good lunch at his place, what remained of the afternoon was spent in torpor. As he sat, *pastis* in hand, at the bar, next to a bust of

Napoleon, he looked the part of the seedy Corsican adrift in the tropics. There was always a Gitane in his mouth and a woman in the background, but Dominique was really in love with the *patronne* of La Casita, one of Saigon's finest French restaurants, as many journalists were in love with her delicious and untouchable daughter Mireille. Early in the war, the *patronne*'s first husband, a Frenchman, had been shot dead by the Viet Cong while out duck-shooting amid the reeds on the other side of the Saigon river. Relations between Dominique and Madame tended to be volatile; I remember the day she rushed into his restaurant, her beautiful face distorted with rage, hurled dozens of plates at the wall, then, without a backward glance, stormed out into the street. She chose suddenly to marry a dull Swiss working for the Red Cross and disappeared to Africa, where it was rumoured she had opened a new Casita in Kinshasa (I have never found it). Poor Dominique was inconsolable. To block the sorrow, he downed an enormous quantity of *pastis*. But like Jacqueline, like Monsieur Ottavj, Saigon was his life; it was impossible to imagine him in any other place. I met him years later in Corsica; he was a forlorn man.

Months of war went by. In April 1972, the North Vietnamese launched their big Easter offensive, overrunning Quang Tri and rolling down almost to the gates of Hué. North of Saigon, too, on Highway Thirteen to An Loc, the fighting was fierce. The last American combat troops had been withdrawn by now, but US officers were still in the field advising the South Vietnamese. Sometimes they died. On 19 June, Lieutenant-Colonel Burr McBride Willey was killed by a rocket on Highway Thirteen. Moose, his faithful grey mongrel dog who was always at his side, was killed too. He had been a man to admire and respect; brave, decent with a conception of duty which responded instinctively to the needs and welfare of the South Vietnamese soldiers and put new heart in them. At this juncture, when the Americans were going home, Willey's death was even more a sad and useless waste. Another American legend, John Paul Vann, who had foreseen the disastrous consequences of the US involvement in Vietnam was also killed that year, when his helicopter crashed on a night mission in the Central Highlands.

Towards the end of 1972, I was recalled to Paris, my assignment over. I resolved it would not be for long. I toyed with applying for a job in Fleet Street. But I knew I had to return to Indo-China. I had passed the best times of my life there; I had been at the centre of the world and I had found harmony between myself and outside events. There was also the unresolved matter of Jacqueline.

The lure of Indo-China was that of a young enchantress. I was bewitched and could no longer resist. It was impossible to imagine that I could ever be happier. So one day I handed in my notice to Agence France-Presse and caught a plane back to Saigon as a near-penniless freelance. The BBC World Service promised that its Vietnamese Service would take three pieces a week from me, and that was it. This provided a weekly income of twenty-one pounds, about enough to take care of my rent. I was confident the rest would look after itself.

By the time I got back to Saigon early in 1973, the Americans had declared that the Vietnam War was over. On 28 January, Dr Henry Kissinger and Hanoi's Le Duc Tho had signed the Peace Accords in Paris. The plea from President Thieu that there could be no peace until there was a full withdrawal of North Vietnamese troops from South Vietnam was overruled. There was to be a ceasefire in place.

It had been a long war, and now the Americans wanted to wrap it up. The first American casualty of the war had been Tom Davis, a twenty-five-year-old adviser, killed as long ago as December 1961. He had been ambushed in the Plain of Reeds, west of Saigon. A shot pierced his head. It was his first Christmas away from his wife and baby daughter in Livingston, Tennessee. Since then, more than 55,000 Americans had died – half of them seventeen or eighteen years old – and 200,000 had been wounded. Davis's name had been long forgotten.

The last American troops pulled out. Prisoners were exchanged, and Kissinger said: 'It is clear that whether this agreement brings a lasting peace or not depends not only on its provisions, but also on the spirit in which it is implemented.' The Vietnamese continued dying at the rate of more than 1000 a week. The grieving went on. A closer scrutiny of this sad piece of arithmetic showed that more Vietnamese were being killed in the post-ceasefire fighting than GIs had been sacrificed by the US in a decade of full-blown war.

The statistic did not escape President Thieu. The world, he told his people in a broadcast from his palace, had washed its hands of Vietnam. It no longer cared.

South Vietnam's national war cemetery at Bien Hoa, twelve miles from Saigon, covered many acres of ground between a crowded four-lane American-built highway and a cement works. It held more than 12,000 soldiers' graves, a fraction of the nation's war dead. But every day it grew larger, as ten new graves were dug. The air was loud with the wailing of widows and the crying of children, and through the sobs could be heard the dull 'thud-thud' of spades digging more graves for the next day's bodies. The ceasefire failed to change the complexion of this cold corner of Vietnam.

The cemetery is still there today, unkempt and overgrown, its graves desecrated by the communists after their final victory in 1975. Many of the dead ARVN soldiers had their photographs engraved on the headstones. The communists smashed these with rifle butts, even shooting out the eyes – a dismal testimony of the hatred generated by more than thirty years of war.

One day I travelled up to the Central Highlands, a place of hypnotic beauty, 300 miles north of Saigon. I wanted to find out how the 'peace' looked for the typical soldier in the 1.1 million strong army of South Vietnam. I found that the war was as sad and brutal as ever, despite the official ceasefire and US departure. It was also a good deal more dangerous. After the US withdrawal, ARVN could no longer rely on the vast array of America weaponry to get it out of trouble. Its soldiers had to fight every battle on their own and for the first time in years ARVN generals had to be mean-minded, drastically limiting the use of artillery and air-supported armour as back-up.

In the Central Highlands, I flew by helicopter from Pleiku to Tango Four, a South Vietnamese firebase clinging to a rain-soaked ridge north of Kontum city, on the fringes of communist-controlled territory. I stayed several days. It was held by the second battalion of the 23rd Ranger Group.

At six in the morning, the outlines of the firebase were dim and hazy. The soldiers, wet and cold, were just emerging from bunkers ankle-deep in muddy water. The guns were hushed. Then, as the layers of early morning mist faded and the day got underway, so too did the war. Fifteen rangers shouldered M16 rifles, machine guns, packs, ammunition; and, with hardly a word of farewell, slipped out of the camp. Seconds after they had passed beyond the safety of the barbed wire perimeter and bamboo palisade (a quaint hangover from the Indo-China war), the patrol vanished like a green serpent into the jungle.

Its departure was watched with anxiety. Tango Five, the nearest outpost on a hill across the valley floor, had been heavily shelled during the night. Communist pressure in the sensitive Kontum area was mounting and the chances of the patrol returning intact to base were slim.

One member of the patrol was Pham Van Nu. He had been presented to me as the typical, simple ARVN soldier in the field. It was a reasonable choice. Like the majority of the garrison, Nu was a teenager, a boyish nineteen-year-old with a winning smile, one of a family of nine. His father, a policeman, had been assassinated by the Viet Cong. His mother struggled to raise the family alone. It was a common tale.

Nu said he had already served two years in the army, and his ambition was to survive long enough to see real peace in his country. It seemed a natural sentiment and doubtless it was shared by countless communist soldiers in the vastness of the jungle all around.

Major Xuong, Tango Four's commander, said that daily patrols were vital. The North Vietnamese were in great strength in the area and would bring up their guns and shell the outpost unless countermeasures were taken.

Tango Four presented a totally different picture from the spic-and-span camps at the rear. The soldiers' uniforms were torn and tattered; boots, vital in this rugged terrain, were holed or simply non-existent. Home for Nu and his friends was a grubby foxhole in the malaria-ridden jungle or a bunker in a squalid outpost with the rats and the stars for company.

They were allowed only seven days of home leave a year; their pay of about ten pounds a month, plus a special rice allowance, was insufficient to buy the essentials of life. If they were thrifty or lucky, the few *piastres* saved from it might keep their sisters off the streets or pay for their younger brothers' education.

What depressed them most was that, once drafted, they were in the army for life. Unlike American GIs, there was no light at the end of the tunnel, no magic demob day.

For much of the morning, the garrison of Tango Four worked tolerably hard. They cleaned their weapons, dug bunkers or felled tall trees outside the perimeter. The trees were to be used as roofing for the new and deep bunker Major Xuong had ordered to be dug in the centre of the camp. The present bunker's roof had crumbled away in the rain.

Other occupants of the camp, however, suspected that the commander's young and attractive wife lay behind this enterprise. The major had won considerable respect by smuggling her onto the base. With the breeze softly stirring her pink pyjamas, she brought a welcome touch of femininity to a drab and spartan camp. There was no trace of animosity over her presence, but the Rangers were saying that the deep bunker would be used to make what they called Number One Love.

Midday came. Everyone took a short break for lunch. The men

ate squatting on the brick-red ground. Major Xuong and the officers ate in a tiny, plaited-bamboo hut with ammunition boxes as chairs. Then, as the major poured tea out of an exquisite porcelain teapot into exquisite thimble-sized cups, shooting broke out in the jungle below.

The effect was electric. The camp's mortars opened fire, its radios crackled and salvos of high-explosive shells from the big guns protecting Kontum city sighed overhead, to burst with angry roars in the forest.

It was an illuminating thought that every shell fired in the war cost as much as thirty pounds, considerably more than Major Xuong or any of his officers earned in a month.

By and by, members of the ambushed patrol drifted into the camp, drenched in sweat, almost insensible with fatigue. They carried a soldier wrapped in a hammock, suspended from a pole. This sad bundle was Private Nu. He was not quite dead, but he was close to it. Blood oozed out of a deep head-wound caused by a mortar bomb which had blown up in his face. He breathed with great difficulty, in short rasping gasps.

Nu lay there on a makeshift bed in the open air as the camp's doctor worked like a madman with his pitifully inadequate medical supplies. Once, I detected a ghost of a smile play over his pale lips. Then it was gone. For hours he hovered between life and death, awaiting the arrival of a helicopter to evacuate him to the field hospital only eight miles away. It ought to have come. They always used to during the big American war, when choppers were two-a-penny and every American soldier knew that he was never more than a thirty-minute chopper ride from an operating table if he was hit. But the priorities were often different now. This was an all-Vietnamese war and choppers were luxuries. None came.

Firebase Tango Four was a most depressing place to be that night. It rained in driving sheets. Thunder rolled round the hills and there was something very eerie about the outpost under the sinister light of the illumination flares. It was shiveringly cold. Everyone was wet, especially Private Nu, who lay unconscious on his bed under a flimsy canvas roof, watched over by the faithful doctor.

Early the next morning we departed on the same helicopter, Nu and I. He, wrapped in a neatly labelled plastic body bag, was bound for the morgue; I was returning to the many delights of Saigon. The nasty little ambush that had cut short his life was not mentioned in any military communiqués. But it would not be forgotten by any of us who had shared his dreadful final night.

The American peace had not even bought a breathing space; the war was still killing boys like Nu every day. It was the loneliest of deaths and on the helicopter ride through the silver mists of that Central Highlands morning, I sat next to Nu's pitiful, zippered-up remains and my sadness gave place to bitterness and gall. By such events, one knew that there was still a war in Vietnam, whatever the rest of the world wanted to believe.

> Each of us
> is a can of tomato paste
> and though we may all
> not have the same label
> as we spin through the air
> when we land too hard
> or get torn,
> from the outside or within,

85

we spill out
and stain the hands of everyone
who knew us . . .

River Ambush

It was 1974. Four hard years of war had passed in Cambodia. Virtually all that was left now of Lon Nol's regime was the city of Phnom Penh and a few enclaves. Any hope of his exhausted army ever winning back the two-thirds of the countryside now in Khmer Rouge hands was out of the question.

There was a terminal smell about the city, a mood of disenchantment, of never-ending siege. The feeling first declared itself on arrival at Pochentong airport. The hot tarmac was thick with planes. Even as the Air Cambodia Caravelle taxied to a halt, tiny propeller-driven T28s of the Cambodian air force, bombs tucked under their wings, roared down the runway on another bombing mission. Warming up behind them were the DC3s and DC4s of Cambodia's many private airlines which thrived on flying food into the city because the main supply roads had been cut.

The five-mile drive into the centre was made a hazard by huge ammunition lorries hurtling through the confused streams of traffic. Every off-duty soldier seemed to carry a gun, and a couple of grenades slung on his belt for good measure.

The city was wrapped in barbed wire. Foreign embassies were walled with sandbags and wire-mesh screens to protect them from the rockets which fell from time to time. American diplomats drove around in bullet-proof limousines. There was a 9p.m. curfew and all but a few restaurants closed two days a week because of a meat shortage.

Only at the Hôtel Le Phnom was there still something of the lazy charm of the pre-war days. But with a difference: most of the French community had deserted the city after the Khmer Rouge shelled it with artillery, hitting the Lycée Descartes.

Albert Spaccessi, the portly *patron* of the Café de Paris, was one of the few old Indo-China hands who refused to leave. He had spent nearly forty of his sixty-one years in Indo-China. His daughter was a pupil at the school. Sipping cognac, the price of which had increased eight times in four years, he said: 'It used to be said Frenchmen were a courageous lot. That's not true any more. One rocket. *Et pouf!* Everyone is leaving. It is ridiculous.'

And while the wretched Cambodian soldiers squatted in their foxholes, fighting to keep the Khmer Rouge out of the capital, some of Lon Nol's top brass could be seen banqueting beside the hotel pool.

One day, I drove down every one of the seven main roads radiating out of Phnom Penh to look at the front lines. It had always been a sprawling city, but the first few miles reflected the disintegration of people's lives. Miserable shanty towns had sprung up on its edges like giant fungi. As much as one-third of Cambodia's population of seven million was now living within the city's boundaries, imposing a severe strain on resources.

Scars of war flashed past; palm trees shrivelled black by napalm, wooden houses burnt to cinders. The further I went, the starker the desolation became. Heaps of rubble and mounds of ashes marked where towns and villages with pretty names once stood. Only twelve miles down one road, and fourteen down another, I came face-to-face with the war: grinning boy soldiers clad in jungle greens and sandals, standing at the side of the road.

A mortar was popping in the background and there were occasional bursts of fire. Girl soldiers in floppy hats twittered shyly from behind an armoured personnel carrier. The colonel was asleep in a hammock. But the fields around were black with death.

A twenty-one-year-old Australian adventurer, Jeff Niven Neyland, was busy cleaning his M16 rifle between firefights. Cambodia was a far cry from Great Yarmouth, where he claimed he once worked as a skindiver. He said he enjoyed soldiering too. Some people thought the Cambodians liked to have their unpaid mercenary around because his white face drew all the fire.

I felt a terrible hopelessness coming over the city each time I visited it from Saigon during 1974. Soon, all overland routes were cut. The airport was under rocket attack; for re-supply the city depended almost entirely on the convoys which sailed from Saigon up the Mekong. Each had to run a gauntlet of heavy communist fire from both banks before it arrived. Over the past six months, several ships had been sunk and about a dozen seamen killed.

It had long been an ambition of mine to travel on one of these convoys up the river to Phnom Penh. There was no noble reason for risking my neck, but what was happening on the river was too important to ignore. The very survival of the city depended on the ammunition, rice and fuel getting through.

All my approaches to shipping companies in Saigon were rebuffed. The risks were too great to take a journalist, they said. Then, one evening, in the upstairs bar of the Miramar Hotel on Tu Do street, I met Johnny Khoo, the manager of a Singapore-based shipping company. Coherent talk was just possible above the din of the juke-box. A cheery, tubby American was dancing with a prostitute in a tight skirt whose zip had almost surrendered under the pressure of her bottom. Her hair rose like a magnificent black soufflé and she wore too much make-up. The last GIs had left Vietnam with the signing of the peace agreement over a year before but, as in Phnom Penh, there was no shortage of Americans in Saigon making a fast buck out of the war.

Khoo watched from the bar as this bizarre couple rolled around the dance floor. He was tall, thin and had a cognac in his hand; his Singapore voice was curiously refined. I gathered that his company had a freighter on the river run and I could tell that, with a bit more drink, he might be persuaded to let me ride on it. The freighter was a rusty old tub called *Bonanza Three*, built in Osaka in 1957, and now fit only for the scrap-yard. That was the very reason why she had been chosen; she was expendable.

Khoo said it cost £165,000 to insure the boat for each voyage. The insurance rates were the steepest in the world, but he made a profit fluctuating around £17,000 per trip. The US government, still deeply committed to Phnom Penh's survival, made it worth his while to gamble with his ship and the lives of his crew. 'The risks are high but, generally, so are the profits,' he said.

A few mornings later, I found myself joining *Bonanza Three*, moored in the oily waters of the Saigon River.

*

92

The first glimmer of light was announcing another day as I kissed Jacqueline goodbye and slipped out of my little Saigon apartment opposite the Hôpital Grall for the world's most hazardous river journey up the Mekong to Phnom Penh. Softly, I called to the hunched form of the sleeping nightwatchman beneath his mosquito net to open the door. As he drew back the shutters of the iron grille, I gave him a French cigarette for his trouble. He accepted it gratefully. The yellow light of tiny kerosene lamps pricked the darkness, and for a moment I stood on the steps breathing in the night air. A gecko chirped eight times; a good omen.

In a short while, the military convoys, the motor cycles and bicycles would start choking the streets; the beggars and stray children would reappear. But in this precious hour before dawn, Saigon was asleep. For those of us who loved the city this was the best time, when cool breezes rustled the flame trees lining the boulevards and the big 155mm guns of the perimeter bases fell silent. Carrying my rucksack and typewriter, I headed across town for the Saigon river, passing from empty street to empty street. Dim figures were moving on the deck as I was ferried across the scummy water in a small barque.

My welcome aboard was warm. Captain Herri Pentoh, her Indonesian skipper, showed me to my cabin. He was a lean, hard, intense twenty-seven-year-old with long, greasy hair over his shoulders. I had heard he was 'a real crackerjack', who had made several river runs already, and was reassured he would not let us down. Pentoh was touchingly apologetic for my spartan accommodation, the peeling paintwork and the plague of cockroaches which had invaded decks and cabins. He said there was no time to scrub *Bonanza Three* clean. She was a 'warship'. His politeness was unnecessary. The sixty-seven bullet and rocket holes I counted in her hull were a more persuasive testimony than words.

The wheelhouse was protected by a thick wall of sandbags. The journey took us downriver from Saigon to the mouth of the Mekong, then up to Tan Chau, a wealthy South Vietnamese river town near the Cambodian border. This part of the journey was enchanting, trouble-free. We passed through lush, green countryside dotted with bobbing sampans and placid villages which showed Vietnam in a rare and attractive light.

At Tan Chau, the convoy formed up for the dash upriver to Phnom Penh. There was a late-night briefing ashore between the ships' captains and the Cambodian navy which had sent gunboats to escort them up to Phnom Penh. In Tan Chau's pre-dawn gloom, the ships were fuzzy outlines in the darkness. The crew, roused from their slumbers at 5a.m. by a clanging bell, sat around drinking coffee, waiting for the signal to depart.

Captain Pentoh was standing in the wheelhouse, gazing through binoculars at the river bank. He did this awkwardly because his vision was obstructed by the sandbags, but also because he had only one eye.

Without warning, three white signal rockets curved gracefully through the sky – the departure signal. On the ships there was great activity. Anchors were raised, engines started. Ship by ship, the little convoy manoeuvred into mid-channel, a conglomeration of misty shapes cutting through the dark waters of the Mekong. The rhythmic beat of the engines was the only clue to their existence.

Bonanza Three was falling apart. As the voyage upstream progressed, it became apparent that she possessed some magic quality which tied her to her crew. Their affection for her was boundless.

Nor was it misplaced. When the crunch came, she showed herself a gallant ship.

On this occasion, she carried 1600 tons of rice. Her crew was composed of twenty young Indonesians and Thais. Their flak jackets and steel helmets made their slender Asian bodies incongruously chubby. But they were a hard, ragged bunch of volunteers, risking their necks for free board and lodging and 120 dollars a month, including danger pay.

They lived for the moment. Ashore, between trips, they went on bacchanalian drinking sprees, revelling in the bars and brothels of Saigon and Phnom Penh, climbing back aboard in the hot mornings, broke and hungover. But on the voyage they were quiet, well-mannered and sober.

That Captain Pentoh had made the Mekong run for more than two years and survived with nothing worse than a minor arm wound, was clearly of enormous comfort to his crew. In Mekong river circles he was something of a legend, for he had been the skipper of the *Ally*, an ill-fated freighter which the Viet Cong had sunk nine months before in an ambush just outside Tan Chau.

Aboard *Bonanza Three*, the big joke was the loo. Apart from making privacy a farce, fist-sized shrapnel holes in the door and wall made it obvious that using it at the wrong moment could prove fatal for the unwary occupant. Happily, the Khmer Rouge gunners had not yet caught anyone with their pants down.

I inquired about the ship's radio officer. 'He's absent,' I was told. I discovered later that 'absent' was a euphemism. The poor fellow had been killed two months before, blasted in his cabin by a rocket. Members of the crew scooped up the pieces in a plastic bag, and were still trying desperately to erase the event from their minds.

Many lives depended on the convoy being adequately protected. The plans were announced at a special briefing at An Long naval base, near Tan Chau, the night before we sailed. The convoy commander, a smart Cambodian naval officer, confidently told the assembled captains not to worry. He called them 'gentlemen' and gave bland assurances that his twenty to thirty gunboats, backed by planes and artillery, would provide adequate protection. He said Cambodian troops had secured some of the most dangerous parts of the route in a series of amphibious assaults that very morning. The captains, sitting in slacks and sandals opposite him at a green baize table, nodded politely. The doubt showed in their weary faces.

Once inside Cambodia and ploughing up the Mekong at a steady eight knots, it seemed the captain's misgivings of the night before had been misplaced. Both river banks were rich ribbons of green. But in striking contrast to Vietnam, where the Mekong and its lush banks buzzed with small-boat activity, great empty spaces of green slid leisurely by. The rich and varied sampan traffic of South Vietnam, the gnarled fishermen and their conical-hatted women were far behind us. The Cambodian river pilot, taken aboard at Tan Chau that morning, explained that the fishing folk had long since departed, their villages destroyed or insecure, to swell the pathetic ranks of Cambodia's two million war refugees.

The gunboats were already around, quivering with anticipation. They fussed among the cargo ships like worried flocks of geese. Twin-barrelled machine guns mounted on their sharp bows whirled constantly, black snouts sniffing the air. Sometimes they let rip at the river bank.

Bonanza Three's entire crew – with the exception of those deep down in the engine room – were by now tightly jamming the wheelhouse. The crush inside and the sticky heat recalled being stuck in the London tube in a summer rush hour. Those who could squatted on the floor with the ship's mascots, seven dogs, for company. The pilot, erect by the wheel, gave orders in a low, matter-of-fact tone. Otherwise there was silence.

Thus the convoy passed the first big danger point virtually unchallenged. At Peam Chor, fifteen miles beyond the frontier, the Mekong suddenly curves and narrows to a 500-yard channel, an ideal and frequent ambush point. Conspicuous to our straining eyes were the hulks of the two ammunition barges sunk ten days before, during the last run – forlorn pieces of rusting machinery poking out of the sluggish water. We rode past them, the river banks drab and hostile at this point, despite the dazzling sunshine.

The chatter of small arms fire showed that the Khmer Rouge were there somewhere. But we were through, the gunboats darting busily among us, covering our passage with a brisk curtain of fire.

With Neak Leung a fading smudge to stern, the danger seemed over. The convoy had suffered no damage and it was now only thirty miles to Phnom Penh. Even Pentoh relaxed, unzipping his flak jacket and pulling off his helmet. No convoy had been hit on the home run for nearly a year. Bowls of steaming rice and spicy fish appeared from nowhere to be wolfed down by the crew. Spirits rose and someone switched on the radio.

The ambush came suddenly, with a rocket attack on the lead ship, *Monte Cristo*, as she steamed past the Dey Do plywood factory twelve miles from Phnom Penh. From *Bonanza Three*'s wheelhouse, two ships astern, it was impossible to assess the damage. But flames and a feather of black smoke on the *Wing Pengh*, 300 yards in front, showed that she too had been hit.

The instinct for self-preservation at such a time is overwhelming. All of us sheltering in the wheelhouse, knowing that our ship was next in line, unashamedly made ourselves as small a target as we could. The situation was too tense and desperate for chatter. In our ears there was only the pounding of blood. The crew were very still, their big American helmets swamping their tiny heads.

Pentoh dominated the scene, taking the wheel himself and steering an erratic course through the fire. The awful din of battle swirled and eddied around, but all we could see from the wheelhouse was dirty puffs of smoke and splashes of dirt on the river bank as shells struck home.

Machine-gun bullets clanged and rattled off the hull. The gunboats leapt almost vertically through the water, their crouched and helmeted crew drenched in spray, their guns becoming living things in their hands.

In the wheelhouse, the little Cambodian pilot carried on with his instructions, his voice as steady as a rock. Only his delicate fingers, tightly wrapped round a small ivory Buddha, betrayed his fear.

The thump of the ship's engines rose above the noise. The words 'starboard easy' had just left the pilot's lips when the rocket burst aft. The explosion was like a mule kick. No one moved. No one said anything except the battle-hardened skipper. 'Bloody hell, we've been hit,' he said, then looked around, embarrassed.

The battle exploded with renewed fury. Then it receded, leaving a sharp whiff of cordite in the air and an overpowering sense of relief and fatigue. More than anything else in the world, the crew wanted to sleep. In a daze, they lay on the wheelhouse floor, which looked like some strange, heaving animal rising and falling.

It was not until we were safely tied up at Phnom Penh's dirty brown waterfront an hour or so later, that anyone bothered to leave the wheelhouse and inspect the damage. The rocket had missed the steering column by a fraction of an inch; had it hit, *Bonanza Three* would have been circling out of control at a particularly tricky moment. A winch was badly damaged. There were a lot of holes. Nevertheless, *Bonanza Three* had survived yet another Mekong river run.

Flak jackets and helmets were discarded and the crew, beaming with boyish pleasure, lined up next to the damage for a perfect album snap.

Walking about Phnom Penh that evening, I visited the press briefing centre at the Groaning Table Restaurant and Cocktail Lounge; a collection of trestle tables spread beneath an enormous banyan tree in the grounds of Colonel Am Rong's headquarters just off Monivong boulevard. Pinned to the bulletin board was a war communiqué of the Cambodian High Command. Never known for the volume of its information, the notice today was a single sheet of paper and particularly succinct. It said, 'A convoy of five cargo ships, two petrol tankers and three ammunition barges has anchored at the port of Phnom Penh after passing up the Mekong without incident.'

I did not dare show the scruffy piece of paper to the crew. Though, by now, if I knew them at all, they were probably too plastered to care.

Desertion

In early 1975, the wars in Cambodia and Vietnam were coming to their final and cataclysmic ends. The decisive act in Cambodia was the mining of the Mekong in the approach waters to Phnom Penh, preventing shipments of rice and ammunition from reaching the capital. The port had always been one of the most exciting places in the city; now it ground to a halt as the shipping dried up. Stripped of their purpose, the biscuit-coloured buildings along the river front looked sad and forlorn.

Ironically, one mined barge that sunk to the bottom was bringing cases of wine up the river for Walther von Marschall, the West German ambassador. This caused quite a chuckle; the ambassador, an astute observer of the political scene as well as a connoisseur of fine wines, was a favourite with the foreign press. Soon he packed his bags and left, together with most of the western diplomatic corps, with the notable exception of the Americans and the French.

I well remember the day of the final British exodus. Up to then, we had been writing frivolous stories about the British, such as 'Plucky Moira' and 'Brave Beatrice' – the Foreign Office and UN secretaries who stayed on in Phnom Penh when the embassy had advised all British nationals to leave – because of the 'uncertain' security situation. They were the sort of trivia beloved of Fleet Street editors. ' "I'm not frightened," says embassy girl left behind in threatened capital,' was a typical headline in the *Daily Mail*.

An RAF Hercules came from Singapore on a final evacuation flight. As people began to clamber aboard, clutching the single suitcase each was allowed, a salvo of rockets hit Pochentong airport. There was pandemonium. Everyone dived for cover. The exception was Lieutenant-Colonel Michael Dracopoli, the defence attaché, who stood resolutely on the tarmac, the epitome of the unruffled British soldier in a tight spot.

These were some of the lighter moments. Those of us who had been covering the war for any period of time watched as the terror crept ever closer; the despair of the people became daily more visible. Everyone knew in their bones that Lon Nol had lost the war: the unscrupulous generals in their Mercedes; the cyclo-drivers carrying the wounded to hospital; the blind soldier-minstrels wandering the streets; the legless cripples; the fortune-tellers; the women grappling with unaffordable food prices; the shopkeepers; the soldiers; the bargirls. When lightning split the spire of the shrine on the top of the little Phnom hill, the fortune-tellers said it was a bad omen. The city had changed, too: the old French bars were replaced by brash haunts covered in rabbit wire, as in Saigon.

Yet amidst the confusion and suffering, the harried, hungry refugees and the emaciated, starving children, ordinary life had to go on as if no danger threatened.

The city brimmed over with absurdities, among them a bush of marijuana, almost as big as a Christmas tree, at fifty cents; a cinema was showing a Swedish film whose publicity advertised it as 'un vrai sexy – cent pour cent d'une qualité sérieuse'. Our guides giggled like children at the novel sight of journalists making the dangerous airport run in helmets and flak jackets. At the O-Russey open air market in the central area, women in long coloured sarongs slowly went about, doing their shopping among the flying splinters of the falling rockets. Ten rockets at least were coming in every day, but the women had no choice but to go outside if they were to feed their families. Food was now so expensive and in such short supply that some families were selling their children. There was a brisk and illegal trade in Cambodian babies to families in the West.

Typical were two little Cambodian girls I got to know – Tiep Bunnary, aged seven, and six-year-old Salroth Thida – due to be adopted by a couple in Britain. Their short lives were already scarred by tragedy. Tiep's father had been killed early in the war, and her mother had cancer and had been given six months to live. Salroth's mother had disappeared a few months before, on a visit to a Khmer Rouge zone, and was presumed dead. An aunt who then looked after her and her six brothers and sisters had died of a heart attack, leaving her father, a wretched army lieutenant earning £5 a month, responsible for seven children.

At first, he did not want to talk about it, embarrassed. Then he said he felt he had no choice but to sell his entire family. 'I love each of my children very much, but I cannot feed them properly. It is heartbreaking to hear them cry out with hunger at night. For their happiness, I wish them all to be adopted.'

A few days before I met them, a rocket burst on the roof of the house, tearing a jagged hole in the ceiling and killing Salroth's best friend. The two girls spoke only two words of English – 'Okay' and 'Bye-bye'. Their broken English and the tears made this scene unbearable. They were being adopted by Kenneth and Margaret

105

Elder, a thirty-nine-year-old engineering works foreman and his wife from Cleveland in the north of England, decent folk with the best of motives, I am sure. But at the time, it was sickening to see the terrible choices being forced on Cambodian families. They were being broken up and sold, like at an auction, brothers and sisters separated and scattered across the globe to find new owners as if on a whim. I worried, too, because I had detected signs of western arrogance and a sense of cultural superiority in these adoption programmes, an unjustifiable belief that somehow we Europeans in the West were more capable of caring for and loving children than impoverished Asians. In this case, it was an uncharitable thought. But I imagined the two little girls growing up in the coal-smudged drizzle of a north of England town instead of the breathtaking greenness of Cambodia. But, in view of what happened, I wish more children had got out, and especially these two little girls.

It was all a wasted effort. The Elders never got Tiep Bunnary and Salroth Thida. There were months of form-filling and large sums to be paid in bribes for exit visas and passports, and the Cambodian authorities even demanded that the prospective parents' income had to be at least twice Britain's national average. By the time these arcane formalities were complete, it was too late. Phnom Penh fell and the children were deported into the countryside by the Khmer Rouge. It is doubtful whether they survived.

The hospitals were heaving with the wounded. Preah Ket Mealea, the main hospital, had four surgeons to operate on 1500 surgical cases, and each day, another hundred casualties arrived from the fighting. There were not enough beds to go round. Many of the wounded lay on straw mats in the corridors. Some of the wounded spent six months on a mat with suppurating wounds, eventually dying. In a sophisticated western hospital, they would probably have been discharged within two weeks. The standard of surgery was often appalling and there was virtually no post-operative care. The surgeons were in such a hurry that they amputated as a matter of course. Wounds burst open so often that they had to be held together with wire. The Olympic Stadium was converted into a casualty receiving centre. But as the wounded poured in by the lorryload the operating triage system was overwhelmed. A sea of stretchers covered the grounds. The dead piled up with the wounded. Young doctors and medical students knelt over the bodies in the intense heat, choosing who was worth operating on, who could wait for surgery, who was a wasted effort.

Here, one day, I watched Cambodia's best surgeon Trang Ky operate on a soldier with a gaping stomach wound. Today, it might seem a ghoulish thing to do. But I needed to know how a surgeon coped in these circumstances. There was a suspicion that an unexploded M79 grenade might have lodged inside. Without caring a jot for his safety, Ky plunged his hands inside the man's belly and poked about in the mangled tissues. It was the hottest month of the year and very sultry. There was no air-conditioning and rivulets of sweat slid down his face. He protected the upper part of his body with a flak jacket, but his hands and arms were fully exposed. As he pulled a silvery string of intestines out of the wound and dropped it like slops in a bucket, he recited Shakespeare, Ariel's song from *The Tempest*.

> Hark, hark! I hear
> The strain of strutting chanticlere
> Cry, Cock-a-doodle-doo

It was his way of releasing tension. Suddenly he pulled out a jagged lump of metal and, uncertain whether it was a bomb, rushed out of the theatre and hurled it from the balcony to the wasteland below. It was the tail-fin of a 60mm mortar and non-explosive, but the operation might have cost him his hands.

I tried to visit this wounded soldier every day. He was making a slow but steady recovery from the hideous wound. Ky said it was a miracle he had survived at all given his condition and the fact that it had taken a day to evacuate him from the battlefield and bring him in. There is a medical rule that the chance of survival from a stomach wound decreases by at least fifty per cent if surgery is delayed by more than twelve hours. But many Cambodian soldiers had the constitution of oxen. Anaemic almost from birth, through disease, their bodies were often better equipped to endure the trauma of major surgery than westerners and they could survive being pepped up with less blood.

Which was just as well. There was a desperate shortage of blood. And, when a newly arrived and well-meaning western surgical team gave a twenty-one-litre transfusion to a woman bleeding heavily, as it would have done in any European hospital, it used up the hospital's entire supply, with fatal consequences for the other casualties bleeding in the corridors.

The woman died of her wounds that night. I felt her death personally; I had accompanied her to the hospital from where she had been hit by a rocket on the city perimeter. Her husband was killed instantly. She was rolled in a rush mat and dragged onto Highway Five. Don McCullin photographed her terribly wounded body as she lay on the road, punctured with shrapnel, with blood so thick that it stuck on her clothes like jelly.

Everyone involved felt very downcast. Ky's brave operation on the soldier also proved a tragic waste of time. He was making a fair recovery, sitting up in bed and with such a vigorous will to live that he would probably pull through. Then Phnom Penh fell. The Khmer Rouge tipped him out into the street where he surely perished; I hope quickly and painlessly, but I doubt it. He deserved a better end. He was an example of the tenacity with which ordinary Cambodians held on to life amid the disintegration of their country and culture.

The hospitals were just one indication of the misery hanging over Phnom Penh. Malnutrition was another; a rapidly spreading cancer which the governments of Cambodia and the United States failed to recognise. We saw it most clearly at the Cambodiana, an unfinished structure, which was to have been a luxurious hotel, one of Sihanouk's last follies before his overthrow. It stood in a garden on the banks of the Mekong and was jammed solid with refugees who had erected scores of shelters in its lobbies. Dr Penelope Key, a nutritionist from Newton Abbot in Devon who had worked among refugees for eighteen months, ran a clinic here. She dealt with thirty or forty cases of kwashiorkor – severe starvation – a day. She did not even see the worst cases, because the children died. 'After four years of deprivation of proteins and vitamins, the children have got to the state where they are on the brink of a precipice,' she said. 'Many are falling over. Every child here is a disaster who has no future as long as the war goes on.'

Then, selecting a baby at random, all belly and matchstick bones, she popped him into the weighing basket. He weighed 14.7lb, the weight of an average British baby at six months – but this child was four years old. Even so his condition was still not yet desperate enough for Dr Key to admit him to her special malnutrition centre at Tuol Kork in the suburbs. Word of this centre spread like wildfire through the foyers of misery in the city. Desperate mothers, whose husbands had been killed, or were in the army and could not provide enough money to feed the family, were abandoning their babies at its gates.

One sad day, I accompanied a US congressional delegation which spent eight hours in Phnom Penh to evaluate the wisdom of pouring in more military aid. It visited Dr Key's malnutrition centre. One member, Bella Abzug, stood in the middle of the cots of dying children and began to cry. She left still in tears. But few Cambodians were sophisticated enough to understand the finer points of the debate in Washington over whether to continue to support the corrupt and crumbling government of Lon Nol. By now, boys who could hardly support the weight of their equipment were being forced to fight.

All the animal vitality that had made even the poorest peasants seem as noble as their magnificent ancestors at Angkor had been extinguished by the war; the grotesque, shrivelled children at Dr Key's clinic reminded me of the last withered fruit on a stricken tree.

The bombardments were so intense that journalists abandoned their rooms at the top of Le Phnom, which were fully exposed to rocket and artillery fire, for those on lower floors. Monsieur Loup, the proprietor, offered the higher rooms for US$5, but even at that knock-down price he had few takers. We rose with the sun and worked all day. The heat at night was suffocating and the electricity was always failing. We learned to write by torch and candlelight and our nights were disturbed by more gunfire and bombardments than ever.

At the beginning of March, Lon Nol, whom the Americans had never liked but found themselves saddled with, was persuaded to leave the country in the hope that his departure would facilitate a ceasefire. The US began last-minute negotiations with Prince Sihanouk, in Peking, which came to nothing. Inexorably, as the end drew near, our Cambodian friends and acquaintances looked towards us westerners for comfort and reassurance. There was the staff at the hotel; the telegraphists at the post office who worked tirelessly throughout the hot nights, getting our stories out to the world on an antiquated telex machine; the doctors and nurses; the shop-keepers; the cyclo-drivers; the girlfriends we had accumulated over the years, the Cambodian journalists and helpers who risked their necks working for the western press, often for a derisory reward.

One day, a delicious cyclo-girl called So Pheap connected with my earliest carefree days in Phnom Penh in 1970, came to see me in Le Phnom and told me she was pregnant. 'Bébé Jon,' she said, rubbing the tummy blossoming underneath her sarong. I was sure I was not the father of her child. Still, I had retained a special fondness for her and we had stayed in touch whenever I was in Phnom Penh. However, I soon divined that her real reason for coming round to see me was a visceral fear of what lay round the corner. She sensed departure in the air and needed support. We westerners spelt safety. I did my best to reassure her but I knew I was lying.

Many Cambodian friends and acquaintances were as worried as she was. The US embassy was peddling the line that a Khmer Rouge take-over would be accompanied by communism, anarchy and wholesale slaughter. This was the 'bloodbath theory'; regrettably pooh-poohed by many western correspondents who saw it as a deliberately over-gloomy assessment to serve America's political interests and try to salvage US honour. There were a few who did not want to believe the string of Khmer Rouge atrocities.

It inspired the poet James Fenton, who was then writing for the *New Statesman*, to compose a ditty which we sometimes sang round the pool of Le Phnom. 'Will there be an awful bloodbath when the Khmer Rouge come to town,' it went, to the tune of 'She was poor but she was honest'. These were eerie occasions of forced jollity and horseplay in the pool. Its unfiltered water was badly in need of a change but that did not stop one girl photographer making love to two men on the same night, one in the deep end, one in the shallow, to general applause. The war had become so ugly, and engendered such hatreds on all sides, that I always believed it would end nastily, though nothing prepared me or anyone else for the horrors in store.

The sudden evacuation of most of the diplomats at the French embassy, flown out on only two days' notice, leaving a skeleton staff behind, came as a sharp psychological shock. France's ties with Cambodia went back a long way and their leaving compounded the city's sense of isolation. One surrealistic day, I watched Louis Bardollet, the delightful first secretary at the embassy and an *aficionado* of Chantal's, as he packed in his villa. He fussed around a sitting-room cloudy with Gauloise smoke, supervising the packing of numerous *objets d'art* he had accumulated in three years of service in Phnom Penh. Occasionally, he stopped his pacing to hammer out a tune on a piano with two broken notes. Not far away, the killing went on. The dull thump of the artillery was clearly audible, an evil noise drowning out the piano.

At the 482 *fumerie*, now frequently shut down because of a tightened curfew and threats of violence from the soldiers manning a check-point at the top of the dark lane, Chantal was looking lost and sad. She urged caution, pointing affectionately at the photographs of Kent Potter, Kate Webb and myself which she had faithfully kept pinned on her wall during all these turbulent years. Kent had been killed in Laos, Kate had been captured by the Viet Cong and later released. I was the only unmarked survivor of this founding trio. The wheel of fortune was turning and Chantal suggested my turn might be coming to suffer a *malheur*. 'Fais attention, Jon,' she said, touching my hand. I did not think about it again, but soon I would have cause to remember her words.

I have never seen or heard of Chantal since.

A few days later I flew to Saigon. South Vietnam too was irretrievably defeated and disintegrating. A presidential guard, fixed bayonets gleaming, still stood outside Doc Lap palace, but in the grounds there were anti-aircraft guns and tanks, while planes circled the city and jeeps bristling with guns patrolled the streets. The city had an air of siege. Much of the countryside had been abandoned or had fallen. The familiar northern cities – Quang Tri, Da Nang, Hué – were being rolled up by North Vietnamese armour and millions were in flight from the abandoned Central Highlands. It was a terrible scramble down Highway Nineteen to the coast, through hills redolent with war. The stream of deserting South Vietnamese soldiers and refugees trekked by the old US First Air Cavalry Division base at An Khe, and through the Mang Yang pass where the crumbling

remains of the French army's Groupement Mobile No. 100, annihil-
ated in a 1954 ambush, still littered the scrub on either side of the
road, next to a monument, 'Here soldiers of France and Viet Nam
died for their countries'. The French were buried standing upright,
facing France.

Frequently, the deserters and refugees were ambushed too, and
by the time this exhausted and miserable column reached the coast
at Nha Trang, the crowded, panic-stricken city was about to fall.
Every front was disintegrating and there was nowhere left to go, no
way out except by sea to Cap Saint Jacques, the Mekong Delta
and Saigon. Misery and despair were absolute. I still wonder what
happened to Dai úy Phuoc, the old information officer for Two
Corps who was so well-read, so helpful, and who loved to speak
French with me whenever I visited his Two Corps headquarters in
Pleiku. He can't have had an easy time.

His boss, General Pham Van Phu, was one of the principal actors
in the army's débâcle. There was perhaps a depressing personal
explanation for his panic. As a young man, he had fought with the
French army as a lieutenant in the Fifth Vietnamese Parachute
battalion at Dien Bien Phu and was taken prisoner by the Viet Minh.
The memory of those camps from which only a small number of
prisoners ever returned – 3000 out of 11,000 – must have made him
supremely conscious of death as the communist juggernaut rolled
southwards in 1975 sweeping all before it. Maybe he thought it was
enough to be a prisoner of the communists once in a lifetime; or
maybe it was the humiliation, for he took out his pistol and shot
himself. At least he escaped the fate of other South Vietnamese
generals, who suffered years of incarceration and mistreatment at

114

the hands of the communists in wretched re-education camps. Some of them did not come home either.

In Saigon, tension was rising. The city was stricken with fear. Almost everyone, it seemed, was mourning a family member lost in the general military collapse. One tragedy piled on another. One Friday afternoon, a US air force C5A Galaxy cargo plane filled with nearly 250 babies for adoption in the United States ploughed into a rice field two minutes after take-off from Tan Son Nhut. The pilot reported sudden decompression problems and turned back, but a door blew out and he lost control. The huge plane came down a mile from the air base, burst open and scattered its cargo of dead and injured babies through the mud.

This tragedy put all the others into context; it reinforced the view that the Americans in Vietnam were jinxed, however honourable their motives. It was the final straw. 'Poor Vietnam. What more can they do to you after this?' I remember saying to a colleague.

Few of my friends in the city though yet believed that the war was lost. Having seen death close at hand during the big Viet Cong attack on Saigon during Tet 1968, and survived, they were psychologically unprepared for anything so fatal as a lightning communist victory over the South. Monsieur Ottavj had died a few months before. I am glad he never saw the end. He was buried at the French cemetery at Mac Dinh Chi. After their victory, the communists demolished the graveyards, turning the French cemetery into a park which, with a strong sense of irony, they rechristened Dien Bien Phu Park.

Afterwards Madame Ottavj, his young widow Thai My Le, invited me over to the Hôtel Royal and met me in the lobby with a conspiratorial air. She wanted me to have her husband's opium pipes. I was

115

flattered and imagined inheriting a fine collection of ivory pipes befitting someone who had smoked opium with Graham Greene, had a lifetime addiction and had derived from it so many dreamy hours of pleasure. She emerged from his room with a wooden tool-box. I took it back to my flat and opened it: it contained yards and yards of foul rubber tubing and other odd contraptions which looked more like unmentionable medical paraphernalia than traditional opium pipes.

In truth, Monsieur Ottavj had always dreaded the prospect of one day being forced to leave Saigon and return to his native Corsica where opium was of course illegal (as it was, officially, in Saigon, but nobody minded; after all, it was not so long ago that it was a monopoly under French government control). In preparation for this unhappy day, he had been trying to assemble a pipe which bore no resemblance to the conventional Indo-China opium pipe, with the bulb in the centre, and would not attract the suspicion of the French Customs. In the end, I dumped the box, with all its pipes, behind a cupboard on the landing of my apartment block in the rue Gia Long. For all I know, it may be there still. I have often thought of going back.

Jacqueline, though, knew the end was in sight. She was quieter, more reflective. We used to slip away and eat at Chez Henri, a restaurant unknown outside a tiny French circle. There were four tables in the kitchen of Henri's house where he served good French provincial food – *jambon cru, paté de campagne* and *rognons*. Henri was an ex-legionnaire with a Vietnamese wife who shared the cooking. But now there was nowhere left to forget the war, not even here. The curfew was being vigorously enforced and, returning to Jacqueline's house after dinner, we were stopped everywhere by patrols. Rats scuttled across Thai Lap Thanh, the little street near the waterfront where she lived, and under the parachute flares the city we both loved looked oddly supernatural. Saigon was losing its permanence, in every sense. I wanted Jacqueline to leave and go to France. But she would not leave without her mother and her mother had nowhere in France to go to. In any case, it would be very difficult for either of them to make the transition. On Saturday, 12 April, we heard that the Americans were abandoning Phnom Penh in a helicopter operation; a humiliating end to their five year involvement in Cambodia. John Gunther Dean, the US ambassador – on whom such high hopes for a solution had been pinned, based on the settlement that he had negotiated in Laos, and who had first come to the US as a refugee from Nazi Germany – was helicoptered out of the city by American marines, weeping, the Stars and Stripes folded under his arm.

It was a day I cannot forget and have never been able to get into proper perspective. I decided I had to fly to Bangkok to write a story on the evacuation; there was a flight which would just enable me to meet my Saturday night deadline. It was not really my intention to go back to Cambodia. But, in case it was possible, I spent that last Saturday morning persuading the Cambodian embassy in Saigon to give me a visa; so I suppose there was the germ of an idea in a back corner of my mind. The visa office could not see the sense of it and nor could anyone else. Most western journalists had been evacuated and the Cambodian collapse was imminent. It could only be a matter of hours, days at the most, before the Khmer Rouge guerrillas would overrun Phnom Penh, and the American warning of a 'bloodbath' was in everyone's minds. The airport was closed, and it was unlikely that there would be any more inward flights, certainly not by civilian airliner from Bangkok: with the city about to fall, it was too dangerous. But the embassy gave me a visa anyway, the last issued anywhere in the world by the crumbling Lon Nol regime.

I hardly imagined I would miss the fall of Saigon, or I would not have left Vietnam that day. It was too precious to me. But Jacqueline knew and implored me not to leave. Her emotion was all the stronger since we had just learned of the death of Michel Laurent in fighting near Saigon. Michel was a fine photographer and the last journalist to be killed in the war. And Jacqueline knew intuitively that I would feel compelled, once in Thailand, to try to go back into Cambodia, the place where Claude had died.

We had been together nearly five years but she had never used the expression 'Adieu, Jon' to say goodbye to me before; a French girl never says Adieu to her lover unless she wishes to mark a definitive separation. I looked back at her standing on the steps of the Caravelle Hotel, not knowing what to think or say, and all the way to the airport her Adieu repeated itself in my mind like a lost refrain and was like a dagger-prick to the heart.

Eighteen days later, she was swallowed up in the communist capture of Saigon; I was trapped in the fall of Phnom Penh and facing my own personal anguish. It had been an act of desertion, of her and of her mother, and it was ten years before I could face going back to Saigon, so intense was the pain from that parting.

The Fall of Phnom Penh

It was not simply journalistic ambition that led me to go back to Phnom Penh, nor was it a zest for adventure. I have pondered on it a great deal since then and of those two facts I am certain. Yet, I still find it impossible to analyse my own motives for my action. Most western journalists had been evacuated to Thailand in US marine helicopters the day before; but here, a few hours later, I was contemplating travelling the other way, back into besieged Phnom Penh, on the last flight before the city fell.

I arrived in Bangkok from Saigon and after filing a story on the humiliating American abandonment of Cambodia I spent sleepless hours in an agony of indecision, my mind racing with emotional thoughts about the doom gathering over Indo-China.

It was well past three in the morning and in a few hours (at 10 a.m. according to the timetable) an Air Cambodge flight was due to leave Bangkok for the Cambodian capital, the last international carrier flying in. There was every chance the flight would be cancelled; the frightened and rational side of my being very much wished that it would be.

But another side of me got the upper hand and, with dawn streaking the sky, an irresistible impulse propelled me out of the

121

security of my hotel room that Sunday morning, into a taxi and to the airport, just in case the plane – any plane – was going to Phnom Penh.

I took almost no clothes; just my Olivetti portable and a camera. These were the same two journalistic implements I had arrived in Phnom Penh with from Paris five years before.

Cambodia had given me so much. In Phnom Penh, I had lived through intensity and exaltation I had never before known. Now that the dream was ending, I had no moral choice but to share its fate. I had a visa. I even had an old Air Cambodge ticket. If there was a plane, I had to be on it; otherwise, I could never look comfortably in a shaving mirror again. I knew I would always be haunted by that cowardice.

There was a plane. And I was on it.

It was an old and overworked DC7 flown by a daredevil American adventurer named Rakar. He was determined to fly into Phnom Penh to rescue his trapped Cambodian girlfriend. At Bangkok airport, however, early that Sunday morning, I had been told emphatically that there was no such thing as a plane for Phnom Penh. Then I was told one had just left. In desperation, I asked the ground staff to get clarification from the control tower. To my astonishment, joy and certainly alarm, I was told that a DC7 was at the end of the runway, on hold because of a fault in its number three engine.

Using all the persuasion I could muster, I got myself whisked through immigration and on a special airport bus to the foot of the plane. The doors swung open. A ladder was lowered. I clambered aboard. I was in the nick of time. Moments later Rakar lined up on the runway, revved the three good engines, released the brakes and, with a rumble, we took off.

It was an astonishing journey of tranquil normality. A smiling Cambodian stewardess served champagne and *petits fours*, as usual. Also on board were Jean-Jacques Cazaux, an old colleague from Agence France-Presse who had been sent back by his office, and Erich Stange, an odiously smug East German diplomat who was going back to reopen his embassy now that a communist victory was imminent. Unlike most countries, France never completely abandoned her embassy in Phnom Penh, counting on her links to Sihanouk and a long history with Cambodia to guarantee the safety of French people and a future French role.

After an hour, the plane rumbled low over Pochentong airport. Rakar shouted to hang on. Then we were down. The door opened, and hard sunlight penetrated the cabin. We had landed in the middle of a rocket and artillery barrage and, scrambling out of the plane, we raced across the tarmac and dived into a sandbagged bunker.

All around was chaos and terror. A frightened crowd mobbed the plane. How many scrambled aboard I do not know, but the aircraft did not hang about. Swinging around wildly it shook off the crowd, waggled its flaps, and was gone; Rakar's girlfriend in the cockpit with him, I hope. Seldom has an airfield felt lonelier than Pochentong did that April morning, as our last link with the outside world rose into the sky, shrunk to a dot, then vanished into the clouds.

I felt a curious sense of relief at being back where I belonged; in a dangerous place, perhaps never more dangerous than then, but one I was familiar with, whose terms of reference I understood. In short, I was at home, and my eyes thrilled at the sight of the frangipani, laden with blossom, on the airport road. My spirits rose at the thought that there were some things, like the fantastic flowers, the dawns over the Mekong, that even war could not despoil.

Nevertheless, I was comforted to see familiar faces at Hôtel Le Phnom. There was Sydney Schanberg, the *New York Times* correspondent, and Dith Pran, his interpreter and guide. Sydney did not join the American evacuation even though his paper asked him to do so. He sent a cable saying, in effect, that he had decided for personal reasons to stay in Phnom Penh. The *NYT* sent back a message endorsing his action and concluding 'We Love You'. Other faces came crowding in, puzzled to see me, but not entirely surprised. There were about a dozen western journalists who had missed the American evacuation for a variety of reasons. They were a diverse group, including the often-wounded freelance photographer Al Rockoff, a former GI from Vietnam who was on about the sixth of his nine lives. Some, like Denis Cameron and Lee Rudekevich, were there rescuing children, and felt their involvement in a baby adoption programme obliged them to stay and protect their charges. The majority, however, were French, reliant on their nationality as a safeguard. Others included Ennio Iacobucci, an Italian photographer friend who did work for AFP; Doug Sapper, a redoubtable American mercenary-cum-businessman involved in a private air charter business to Battambang, the second city; Dominique Borella, a tall, blond French soldier-of-fortune who had made the Cambodian cause his own and had attached himself at the head of a battalion of parachutists defending the airport. There were also the Cambodian journalists and stringers, with whom I was united by five years of shared dangers on the battlefield, in particular the loyal Moonface.

Five other Britons had stayed behind: a Scottish medical team brought out by the Red Cross to alleviate some of the misery in the city's primitive, overcrowded hospitals – Helen Fraser and Pat Ash, nurses; Michael Daly, surgeon; Murray Carmichael, anaesthetist – and Major 'Spots' Leopard, field director of the Save the Children Fund.

In the past we had been somewhat cut off from the war in the Hôtel Le Phnom – not any more. The façade of the old colonial building was bedecked with giant white flags and red crosses and surrounded with barbed-wire barricades. It had been declared a 'neutral zone' by the Red Cross. Outside, however, a squadron of armoured personnel carriers squatted menacingly on the wide avenue, arousing fear that the government might be setting a strong-point up around the hotel in defence of the city. The Red Cross finally got assurance that its neutrality would be respected and it would be left in peace.

Monday was Cambodian New Year. There were no celebrations. A mutinous air-force pilot dropped four bombs on the military headquarters, killing at least seven soldiers. General Sak Sutsakhan, the new military leader, proclaimed a twenty-four-hour curfew and declared the struggle would continue. The Khmer Rouge attacked the western outskirts, driving thousands of refugees towards the city centre. They poured through the military police barricades like floodwater. But other aspects were astonishingly normal. Cyclo-drivers, all smiles in the morning sun, glided past while the government news agency ignored the imminent defeat and carried a big story about the death of the singer Josephine Baker.

Sydney, Pran, Al and I travelled in a group around the city. We drove to the airport and the main transmitting centre nearby, but it was shut and the technicians had fled. Our dispatches were sent from the post office by an extraordinary emergency transmitter made in China before the fall of Shanghai. Worried it would shut down at any moment, we used to spend the night at the post office, gunfire mingling with the chatter of our portables, handing page after page to the telex operator, who punched it, and fed it down the line to our respective masters in London and New York. None of us got more than an hour or two of snatched sleep, resting our heads on our machines, our bodies dripping in the heat.

By Wednesday, the misery was overwhelming, the gunfire growing louder. A huge fire raged on the southern edge of the city, where thousands of wooden shacks lined the river. Another inferno at the Shell depot lit up the sky to the north. With the US evacuation, the relief organisations had broken down and the refugees had nobody to rely on. A woman came down the airport road dragging a sewing machine, all she had salvaged from her home. In the university grounds, half-tracks churned up the grass and positioned themselves for clearer fields of fire. Troops who had pulled back from the east bank of the Mekong, now entirely in Khmer Rouge hands, thronged the building.

Upstairs, in the Faculty of Medicine, a Para Corps captain, swagger-stick in hand, strode up and down, barking orders. Students had barricaded the stairs with desks and watched the bustle from classroom windows. And in the sunshine outside two young lovers sat on the grass, holding hands, wrapped in their own private world.

On the Monivong Bridge over the Bassac River, the army's 2nd Division under Dien Del, the general with whom I first saw combat five years before, had regrouped. Dien Del strutted up and down in his tiger suit, pistol at his hip, saying he would fight to the last.

126

Looking at me squarely, he said that if taken prisoner he would 'accept the law of the vanquished'.

Nearby was the scene of the previous night's terrible fire. The conglomeration of wooden houses, on stilts near the Bassac's confluence with the Mekong, was caught in Khmer Rouge shelling. As flames spread through the flimsy structures, hundreds were trapped and burned to death. Many more tried to escape by leaping into the water. Naval gunboats, searchlights blazing, manoeuvred among the bobbing bodies, trying to fish out survivors.

There was one place I had to see again before the city fell: the lunatic asylum in the industrial suburb of Tak Mhau, three miles away on the river's edge, which I had visited a few weeks before. What I thought I could do about it, I did not know. It was one of the most heart-wrenching places I had seen. Here, in degrading conditions, lived a group of men and women of differing ages, put away because they had been classed as mentally ill. They were certainly very disturbed and incapable of caring for themselves. Yet, with the buildings trembling from the shock of rockets and shells, one had to ask who was more insane – these pitiful human creatures, one of whom clasped a simply carved wooden figure of a bird in his hand (I like to think it was a dove of peace) – or the soldiers killing each other outside?

My attention was transfixed by a girl who emerged from a small dark room. She was young, scarcely grown up. She was ragged and filthy, but with one of the most enchanting faces I had seen. She moved across the little courtyard with all the gracefulness and guile of a wild animal. She was like a wolf-child. No one spoke to her. Everyone ignored her. When I held out a piece of baguette and some boiled sweets she snatched them from my hand like an animal; then, before she scampered away into a corner to eat them, she smiled. It was a smile to dream about for a long time. I could not find out much about her, except that she had been found demented in a ruined village somewhere along the Mekong. In the terror of that fighting, something in her mind had snapped; she had not uttered a word since.

Now the war had caught up with her again, with a vengeance. As I headed towards the asylum, smoke was rising above the houses and refugees were flowing down the road. I was stopped by soldiers at a barricade and told that Tak Mhau had fallen.

Back at the hotel, rooms were being emptied of arms and even of military souvenirs like rocket fragments, mortar fins, North Vietnamese pith helmets – mementoes amassed by guests over the years. Cambodian officers and other 'non-neutrals' who had moved in with their families and belongings in the hope of escaping Khmer Rouge reprisals, were being expelled by the Red Cross. They left reluctantly.

The Red Cross had given everyone in their 'neutral zone' a list of rules forbidding, among other things, bathing in the swimming pool. It was thought that if there was a prolonged siege, the pool-water – turgid and soupy after months of neglect – might have to be filtered and drunk. The hotel, already out of bread and fresh eggs, was now out of ice. Monsieur Loup was profusely apologetic. 'C'est la guerre,' he said with a wring of his hands, as if anyone didn't know already.

I found the Scottish medical team in a bungalow attached to the hotel which they had converted into an operating theatre complete with half a dozen camp beds. They were exhausted, having spent the blackest day of the war at the Preah Ket Mealea Hospital. In two hours in the morning they had performed ten operations. 'I didn't have time to put on gloves or a gown. I simply splashed alcohol over my hands and didn't even have time to change the instruments between operations,' said Daly, the Glaswegian surgeon.

The bungalow where the team planned to keep operating to the end was something else. Throwing open a cupboard, Daly claimed he had enough equipment to operate on twelve patients without having to pause even to wash up.

By early evening, the scenes of chaos and horror were mounting. Attempts to confine refugees to the outskirts ceased and they were converging on the centre from all sides, pushing, shoving, jostling, desperate to escape the fighting.

The trim walkways and flower-scented parks were submerged under a heaving mass of homeless families; weeping, lost children; pigs; ducks; chickens; all increasingly afraid. Part of this great crowd saw the Red Cross signs and, assuming our 'neutral zone' was a relief centre, tried to push their way in.

I made my way to the converted volleyball court which served as a receiving centre for the wounded. It was overwhelmed. Uncontrollable shrieks and whimpers of pain rent the sour, fetid air. A dozen doctors and nurses were dealing with more than 700 cases. The chief medic was in despair. The wounded were stacked like logs, two or three to a bed. Blood streaked the floor. The bins overflowed with gory bandages and field dressings. A human leg poked out of a cardboard box where a surgeon had tossed it in a hurry. Its owner lay staring blankly on a stretcher crimson with blood.

A soldier staggered in, glassy-eyed and exhausted, cradling his baby daughter in his arms. He laid her on a bed occupied by a soldier with a mangled foot – laid her gently, almost apologetically, trying not to jolt the soldier. He pulled back the red-checked scarf he had wound round her little head and his young face collapsed as he saw she had already died – a lump of rocket had torn a hole through her.

I was overdosing on horror and headed back to the hotel, straight into a deeply unpleasant argument. A few of the French *colons* and journalists could not stomach the prospect of Le Phnom, this exclusive hangout of foreigners and rich Cambodians, being converted into a refugee camp. They were rudely assailing Red Cross officials for giving refugees shelter in the spacious hotel grounds.

Refugees were being admitted, family by family, after Red Cross officials, with commendable patience, had searched their bodies and belongings for weapons. From under their clothes and from inno-cent-looking bundles, poured out a fantastic array of arms – rifles, pistols, knives, switch-blades, chains, even a knuckleduster. The searchers dumped them in a big wooden box for disposal later. This incredible collection proved that some were army deserters who had quit the battlefield to get their families to safety.

Disarmed, they tramped through the high-ceilinged lobby into the garden on the other side, where they spread out little mats beside the pool and fell into exhausted sleep. A green plastic rod separated them from the handful of westerners dining at La Sirène, the open-air restaurant on the far side of the pool. 'That's what's called apartheid,' said a French journalist, who had been in Johannes-burg. It was not a moment any of us felt proud of.

The protests from the *grands messieurs*, as the Cambodians call westerners, continued. Finally, André Pasquier, the chief Red Cross delegate, lost his temper. Shaking with emotion and fatigue, he told them to shut up. 'If you don't like it,' he said, 'get out.' Few went.

Sydney, Pran and I did not stay at the hotel that last night. We were in the post office, filing, until dawn the next morning. The buildings shuddered from the bombardment but we were oblivious as we concentrated on our work as though possessed, knowing that at any moment communication might go down.

About an hour before dawn, I spoke on the phone for the last time to Long Boret, the prime minister. He was a man without malice and a higher standard of morality than the members of the unscrupulous circus around him. Lon Nol had left for Hawaii with one million dollars. Even as the city was falling we saw a grotesque exchange of telegrams involving the Cambodian National Bank in this payment. Long Boret's responsibility was awesome. He had been determined that the city would not surrender, although its position was hopeless now that America had discontinued its airlift of food, fuel and ammunition. 'I will stay and starve to death with my people,' he had said, but I found him in bad shape, weighed down with despair and exhaustion. 'The military situation has become impossible. We have no more material means. We feel completely abandoned,' he said. 'My first objective now is to end the suffering of the people.' By this time, gun and rocket fire made it possible to communicate only in shouts. Abruptly, I was cut off.

An hour later, the city fell. The chief telex operator, who had worked through the night to send our last dispatches to the world, learned that his little girl had been killed by artillery fire near Chamcar Mon Palace and his wife had been fatally injured. Dressing hurriedly, uttering not a word, he went out. As he passed us, a limp figure in the sunlight, we averted our eyes.

Quickly, we moved back to join the other foreigners in the hotel. The crackle of small-arms fire came closer. From a balcony off Sydney's room on the second floor, we saw soldiers who had thrown away their guns mingling with the refugees streaming into the city from the north. A squadron of armoured personnel carriers regrouped around the hotel. They had come from the collapsed northern front. It was unclear whether they would fight or surrender.

The insurgent radio broadcasting a message 'We are ready to welcome you' was the first sign that the Khmer Rouge were entering the city. Then Pascal, a Red Cross doctor, burst into the hotel lobby, saying insurgents were near the French embassy half a mile down the road. As he raced upstairs for his passport, mortars fell a few streets away. The din of battle mounted to a crescendo and the refugees in the hotel grounds huddled closer together. The government radio began playing French military music, presumably to squeeze a last drop of patriotic fervour. Then it went off the air.

People in the street began to run. White flags sprouted everywhere – on APCs drawn up outside the hotel, on houses in the northern sector of the city which the Khmer Rouge had penetrated. Yellow alamanda blossoms covered the headlamps of the APCs; after five years of war the army was packing up. Troops took out the clips of their M16 rifles and waited quietly in the sunlight.

With fighting noises still coming from the southern part of the city, a crowd gathered on Monivong boulevard outside the French embassy. It stretched across the road and in the centre of it was a young man in black with a flat round face and a white scarf. The soldiers and townspeople around him joined hands, hoisted him on their shoulders and bore him triumphantly to an APC. Western photographers and a mixed group of soldiers and civilians climbed up with this apparent Khmer Rouge soldier. The APC moved down the boulevard, past the Hôtel Le Phnom, seeming to carry a message of peace.

For a moment there was hope. Then a mortar crash tore the air, and there was a splash of smoke up the road. Another mortar bomb burst, closer. A machine gun knocked harshly. The APC slewed round, and roared back the way it had come. We scattered. The Khmer Rouge were welcome in one part of the city but met with force in another.

For twenty minutes, fighting swirled through the streets round the hotel. A Red Cross stretcher team rushed a wounded soldier through the lobby filled with people cowering from stray bullets. Hardly more than a boy, he had a small, black hole in the side of his head.

In the bungalow-cum-operating theatre, Daly took one look and shook his head. 'He has a bullet in the brain. There is nothing we can do.' The soldier coughed up a stream of blood. His hands fluttered. With a shudder, he died. Daly and his team moved on to the next casualty, a civilian with a bullet in the lung.

There was a commotion outside. Prince Sirik Matak was among scores of refugees trying to fight their way into the hotel. Red Cross officials refused him entry on the grounds that his presence would endanger the lives of the others. Matak, Sihanouk's second cousin and a career civil servant, had played a key role in the 1970 coup against the prince and became deputy prime minister under Lon Nol. He was one of the seven 'arch traitors' of the Lon Nol regime, condemned to death by the Khmer Rouge. He spoke briefly to reporters about the fighting. 'You see, these are personalities who are determined to resist. We do not want a communist government here.' In evident distress at being turned away, he left and was granted asylum in the French embassy, but first he handed out a copy of the letter he had written to John Gunther Dean. The ambassador had invited Matak to join the American evacuation the previous Saturday with other Cambodian leaders. He had refused and this is what he wrote:

Dear Excellency and friend,

I thank you very sincerely for your letter and for your offer to transport me towards freedom. I cannot, alas, leave in such a cowardly fashion.

As for you and in particular your great country, I never believed for a moment that you would have this sentiment of abandoning a people which has chosen liberty. You have refused us your protection and we can do nothing about it. You leave and it is my wish that you and your country will find happiness under the sky.

But mark it well that, if I shall die here on the spot and in my country that I love, it is too bad because we are all born and must die one day. I have only committed this mistake in believing in you, the Americans.

Please accept, Excellency, my dear friend, my faithful and friendly sentiments.

Sirik Matak

By and by, the fighting died down in the northern part of the city, and people emerged into the streets. They wore *chromas*, the checked scarves which are a symbol of friendship in rural Cambodia. Soldiers of both sides rode through the streets on the tops of half-tracks. 'Hey, Mister Journalist, take our picture,' they cried. Everyone seemed filled with joy at the end of the war and the dream of peace and freedom.

We saw a smiling monk in saffron robes riding in a jeep with a guerrilla and were told through an interpreter that the new regime would respect Buddhism. Khmer Rouge soldiers, hardly more than boys, were riding around in a host of vehicles including captured ambulances. I walked the quarter of a mile to the post office, only to find it deserted, its communications down. Outside, in the Provence-style square, a Khmer Rouge soldier pedalled by on a bicycle. He wore the usual soft Mao hat, green fatigues and hanging field glasses. The pistol on his belt indicated he was an officer. He smiled politely, but refused our gifts of oranges and cigarettes. 'The corrupt and the traitors will have to be punished,' he said. 'But I can assure you there will be no bloodbath.'

Out at the Olympic Stadium, senior army officers and politicians of the collapsed regime were making their getaway, among them General Sak Sutsakhan, the Supreme Commander, and General Dien Del. The helicopters had been standing by for the last thirty-six hours, fuelled and ready to go. They clattered into the air as the first Khmer Rouge pushed into the stadium, bazookas and rifles at the ready, and flew to Thailand. Notably absent was Long Boret. One story claims that, at the last moment, he left the stadium with his wife and went back to collect some valuables she had left at home. The helicopters had to leave without them. I like to think, however, that he was sincere and, true to his word, stayed behind to hand over the city to the victors and end the bloodshed.

135

Intense fighting continued in the west near the airport, where the crack paratroop brigade was making a final stand. A key figure was Borella, the ex-legionnaire. Powerfully built, larger than life, Borella had been wounded three times in the past six months. He lived and fought with the Cambodian paratroop brigade for very little money. I had met his sort before in the Foreign Legion, very much the adventurer, a man without a country, whose first love was soldiering. He met an agonising end the following year fighting on the Phalangist side in the Lebanese civil war. He was captured and tortured to death. Borella helped direct the last defence of the brigade headquarters on the edge of the airport. When it finally crumbled in the late morning, he shed his uniform. His girlfriend fixed him up with some civilian clothes and, resourceful to the last, he sought refuge in the French embassy. At the Para HQ, the Cambodian brigade commander shot himself.

It now seemed tolerably safe to wander around the central part of town. The Khmer Rouge, who were firmly in control, seemed a friendly bunch. With Sydney, I headed for the Ministry of Information, where we had heard there was a gathering of Khmer Rouge military leaders.

A curious sight greeted us. Holding court on the grass outside the long, colonial-style building, was a young man in black, with a handsome, angular face. In impeccable French, he introduced himself as Hem Ket Dara, son of a former minister, and described himself as the commanding general of a nationalist movement that had 'liberated' the city.

He was twenty-nine, had been educated in Paris, had a French wife in France, and had been in Phnom Penh since 1971. He was not a communist. He had the arrogance of a playboy. There was an air of fantasy about him and it was inconceivable that he could fit the tough mould of the Khmer Rouge. Even his black uniform looked as if it had been tailored by Yves Saint Laurent. He issued orders all the time, telling the young, black-clad soldiers around the building to move back and stay still. When they pushed forward again, he brandished a pistol in Hollywood fashion, which elicited only token respect.

He boasted that he had taken Phnom Penh with only 300 men and had suffered no casualties. Then, dismissing us with a wave of the pistol, he told us to listen to broadcast announcements. 'The city must be reorganised before you can send dispatches,' he said. But he and his soldiers struck a false note. They were too neat and friendly to be genuine Khmer Rouge straight from the hills.

Now, worrying and conflicting reports began to circulate about the identity of these units swirling around town with guns. It seemed there were already at least two factions: those in the north (including the amazing Dara) appeared friendly. Reports from the southern sector of the city, where sporadic fighting still continued, however, told of a very tough force which had moved in and was busy digging foxholes. It was pushing refugees out of the city and seemed to be deploying for battle.

The implication was that the troops in the north were nationalist; those in the south hardline Khmer Rouge. This was probably too simplistic. Dara and his merry band were opportunists who had misjudged the mettle of the Khmer Rouge and were trying to usurp power before they arrived.

Rockoff, the photographer, came back from the southern sector, saying the Khmer Rouge there were grim-faced and seasoned soldiers. Their mudstained feet and uniforms showed they had not been pussyfooting around. They were disarming government soldiers, stacking all weapons into huge piles, throwing away the boots and marching the men out of the city to unknown destinations.

It was 12.30p.m. We now felt secure enough to drive around the northern part of the city. A few of us went to the Preah Ket Mealea Hospital, a gloomy set of buildings five minutes from Le Phnom on the banks of the Mekong, where hundreds of people were being subjected to a hideous death. The doctors had not reported for work for two days. There was no one to treat the 2000 wounded and the plasma bottles and saline drips were emptying one by one.

People were bleeding to death by the dozen in the corridors. The floors of the wards were caked with blood. The hot, fetid air was thick with flies – the sight of these swarming over the living and the dead, over the anguished faces of those who knew they were doomed to die, churned my stomach and made my mind reel. I asked a distraught nurse for an explanation. She said she had phoned the doctors. 'They say they are coming in a short time, but they are not here yet. Maybe they are afraid.'

These scenes of horror wiped out the work of the Scottish team who had filled a downstairs ward with sophisticated equipment and brightened it with children's pictures.

Upstairs was worse. The dead and the dying lay in pools of their own blood. The long corridor outside the operating theatre was literally awash with it. A man and his wife had died in each other's arms. A few feet away, an old man was pushed hard up against the wall, his intestines tumbling out like laundry. Further down the corridor was a soldier with arm, head and stomach wounds – a Khmer Rouge who had somehow been brought in for treatment.

A single harassed doctor fussed about impotently, stethoscope around his neck. It was easy to see that, but for our presence, he would already have gone home. Through fly-blown lips, the Khmer Rouge croaked: 'Water, water, please get me some water.' We could not give him any because of his stomach wound.

Hospital workers with scrubbing-brushes and bowls of soapy water started to wash the blood off the floor. They brushed between the legs of the corpses and sent the red mixture splashing down the open lift shaft. With one accord, Sydney, Al, Pran and I sloshed our way through the blood to the exit and left.

It was one o'clock, the hottest time of the day. We emerged into the oven-like heat to find people edging inside the buildings and running away from the front gate. There was a distinct mood of danger. We drove cautiously through the hospital grounds towards the street, but before we could reach it, there came a rush of footsteps. Half a dozen Khmer Rouge soldiers, bristling with guns, stopped the car, dragged us out and shook their rifles at us. They were boys, some perhaps twelve years old, hardly taller than their tightly held AK47 rifles. Their ignorance and fanaticism made them super-deadly.

Their leader's eyes were coals of hate. He was screaming and ranting, foaming at the mouth. He held his pistol against my head, finger firm on the trigger. My hands were high in the air and I was paralysed with fear. My camera, notebooks and other belongings littered the ground where the Khmer Rouge had thrown them. The seconds ticked by. Pran uttered some soothing words in Khmer. Then I was able to rejoin the others on their side of the car. A chastened, terrified group, we moved under escort to a captured APC in the street outside.

Sydney, Al and I were forced at gunpoint into the back of the APC. The Khmer Rouge told Pran he was free to go; they were only after the 'rich and the bourgeoisie'. He insisted on staying, as did our driver, Sarun. At the last moment, just before the top hatch and rear door were bolted, Pran talked his way inside and joined us. We sat in the gummy heat and waited for them to toss in a grenade and finish us off.

We rode through the streets and stopped to pick up two more prisoners, Cambodians in civilian clothes. The big one with a moustache and a crew-cut wore a white T-shirt and jeans. The smaller man was wearing a sports shirt and slacks. Both were officers and quite as frightened as we were.

The big man was second-in-command of the government navy. He tried to pass us his wallet with his ID card. We whispered that it was no use. Finally he hid it in the back of the APC among some oily rags. The small man put an ivory Buddha in his mouth as a talisman.

Sydney also had a talisman; a crumpled bit of yellow cloth, an artificial rose that had been a gift from his daughter a couple of weeks before. 'As long as I've got this, we will be all right,' he said, forcing a thin smile. I did not share his faith.

I was still young enough to believe that death, even in Cambodia, happens mostly to others. Now I was faced with death myself. I had coped with it a number of times on the battlefield, but this was different. To have my head blown off by a teenage soldier at close range when the war was over seemed a ridiculous, ineffectual and unfair ending to life. I longed to be told it was all make-believe. I cursed myself for ever having left the security of the hotel to see the casualties in the hospital and wished that the clock could be turned back a couple of hours. The same emotions must have run through the minds of all those other journalists in the minutes before they were murdered by the Khmer Rouge.

We were prisoners inside the APC for about twenty-five minutes, sweating like pigs in the heat. But time no longer existed; I was already beginning to feel remote from the world outside. I thought of the wastefulness of my life, the people I loved and would never see again. I prayed softly. I know that I wanted desperately to live but I am struck by our lack of protests or resistance. Of course, they would have done no good. The young Khmer Rouge had eyes as cold as stone and were determined to kill us. We were condemned men. Our deaths would be squalid. But surely we should not have gone like lambs to slaughter.

The top hatch unfolded with a clang and a man pointing a gun at me screamed, 'We are not Vietnamese. We don't like Vietnamese.' It was an odd thing to say. I had been speaking in French only to establish that I was not American. Perhaps he thought I had been talking in Vietnamese. Evidently he harboured the traditional Cambodian hatred for their Vietnamese neighbours.

The wretched minutes ticked by. At 1.40p.m., the APC shuddered to a halt. Bolts slid back. The rear door was opened. I saw water and a pair of Khmer Rouge soldiers, pointing rifles, beckoning us out. We stared at one another. We were sure this was journey's end; we would be executed and our bodies tossed into the Mekong.

Eyes blinking, we stepped into the sunlight. Immediately Pran began to talk. He talked and talked. He spoke softly and firmly, telling the Khmer Rouge that we were neutral journalists, there to witness their historic 'liberation' of Phnom Penh and Cambodia. By and by, the tension went out of the air. We were ordered to stand across the street from the river and wait. We drank water from a bucket and watched people stream out of the city up Route Five.

We assumed they were refugees from the war returning to their homes now the fighting was over. In fact, the Khmer Rouge had issued orders for the entire city to be evacuated. They had also started to loot, a process that continued for days. As we stood there, guerrillas drove past in cars heaped high with cigarettes, soft drinks and wines. Few knew how to drive: the crash of gearboxes was the prevailing sound. In other circumstances, their efforts would have been hilarious; now they were grotesque: the peasant boys with death at the tips of their fingers were behaving like spoilt brats. They seemed every bit as irresponsible as the Cambodian army they had defeated.

At 3.30 a man of authority ordered us to be released, and most of our belongings were returned. The Khmer Rouge kept the car, my notebooks, films and hotel key. We were too tired to argue. Hitching a ride with two Frenchmen, we drove straight to the Ministry of Information, where we understood there was to be a news conference. We left behind the two Cambodian prisoners. I remember them standing limply on the riverbank, beseeching looks in their eyes. They knew they were condemned to die, and there was nothing we could do. We made a feeble sign of pity and abandoned them to their fate.

Talking his way into our APC was a singular act of courage by Pran. His grim loyalty to Sydney, our inability to save him later and his miraculous survival is, of course, now well documented in *The Killing Fields*. Inevitably, I have not seen him for a while, but whenever I have, it has been in Cambodia and a celebration of an old comradeship born in those minutes of extreme danger when we were very close to death. I owed him my life that day.

At the Ministry of Information, the scene was menacing and tense, markedly different from the morning. The hardline Khmer Rouge had now taken over. Dara, the flashy early leader, was there, but he had been disarmed and was a semi-prisoner. The cocky expression had vanished and he looked tired and uneasy. Fifty prisoners were lined up in front of the building. They included Lon Non – Marshal Lon Nol's younger brother and one of the most notoriously corrupt, hated members of the old regime. (I learned later that he was behind Dara's far-fetched attempt to seize power.) There were several generals and the director of Long Boret's cabinet. Of the prime minister himself, there was not yet a sign.

An unidentified youngish man in black, clearly a Khmer Rouge leader, bawled through a bullhorn at the prisoners, dividing them into three groups – military, political and civilians.

The group of guerrillas training their guns on them were tough, strong-looking, in jungle green, soft Mao hats and Ho Chi Minh sandals. Each was a walking arsenal. To us they looked like soldiers from another planet, as vicious as the group who had seized us that afternoon. Their leader talked to the prisoners. He told them there were only seven 'arch traitors' and the others were not captives, but surrendered people. He pledged there would be no reprisals.

As he talked, a squad of soldiers, no more than fourteen years old, crouched in combat positions among the trees, menacing us and the prisoners with their guns. Some were digging weapon pits. Then three old ladies from the Cambodian Red Cross came forward and offered their co-operation. They too might have come from another world, for they were dressed up in their finery – silk sarongs and blouses, silver belts, jasmine in their hair – as if for a party.

The Khmer Rouge leader made a short statement. He said he represented the armed forces and wished to thank all the 'people in the world who love peace and justice', including the American people, for their support. Asked if Americans would be killed, as the US embassy had predicted, he said: 'We respect prisoners of war. That is our military position.' But he did not know what the Khmer Rouge political leaders planned. He was a soldier whose job was to secure the city. The politicians would come later. As he spoke, gunfire still rattled through some quarters.

A few minutes later, a black Citroën pulled up and Long Boret got out, his eyes puffy and red, his face empty of expression. When we asked him how he was, he muttered a short, incoherent sentence. His thoughts were elsewhere. Dazed, legs wobbling, he surrendered to the Khmer Rouge and joined the line of prisoners. I could not fail to admire his courage.

In the hours that followed, the Khmer Rouge killed Long Boret and the other officials whom we saw surrender at the Ministry of Information, probably with extreme brutality.

*

Without warning, Khmer Rouge soldiers forced their way into our quarters at the Hôtel Le Phnom and harshly told André Pasquier of the Red Cross to empty the place within half an hour. Wild soldiers rushed through the Scottish medical team's operating theatre in black hordes, demanding cartons of medicines. They rummaged through the cupboards. They drank the bottles of intravenous serum. One of the nurses stripped a wounded government soldier of his uniform and put it roughly over a dead man. Otherwise the soldier would have been shot.

Pandemonium gripped the hotel. People ran in all directions. What did it mean? Where would they go? The consensus among the foreigners was to seek the security of the French embassy, half a mile down Monivong boulevard. The Cambodian refugees in the garden had no such choice. Gathering their cooking pots, they set out for the countryside. So, too, did the hotel staff who clutched imploringly at our arms. 'Don't abandon us.' Their words come back to haunt me now, for most of them are dead.

It was time to say goodbye to the hotel. Forgetting all thoughts of getting into my room and collecting my belongings – the Khmer Rouge had taken my key anyway – I joined the trail of refugees on the road outside. As we headed along the boulevard towards the embassy, a fresh battalion of troops marched Indian-file into the town. They were well-armed, disciplined, marching with the swagger of victors; soft-faced boys with malevolent eyes which stared straight ahead.

The French embassy was surrounded by a high wall. As dusk closed in on this Thursday, 17 April, people rushed to climb over and into the embassy. In a few seconds, they were scrabbling for a

145

foothold, hanging by their fingertips, passing over their children and belongings in a mad stampede. An Indian fell and broke his leg in the crush. All the while, people were streaming out of the city in their thousands. The darkening street was thick with humans. Abandoned cars, discarded shoes, littered their path.

An unthinking madness was taking over. In its zest for revolution, the Khmer Rouge soldier-peasantry was not embarking on the blood-bath predicted by the Americans. Instead, it was emptying the city of its people. There clearly was a discipline: a cold-blooded discipline which said the Khmer Rouge new order was the only one; that anything in its way had to be eliminated. It was not a discipline which respected human life or property.

Fernand Scheller, chief of the UN Development Project (UNDP) in Phnom Penh, told me, 'What the Khmer Rouge are doing is pure and simple genocide. They will kill more people this way than if there had been fighting in the city. The next rice crop is not until December and anyway, without outside help they can grow only enough to feed thirty per cent of the population.' He had forty-two people standing by in Bangkok to come in. 'I am ready to help them – not them, the people. What is going on now is an example of demagoguery that makes one vomit.'

Scheller nearly wept when his Cambodian family and workers were banished with everyone else to the countryside. 'I have spent the whole day betraying my friends,' he said.

I awoke the next morning to find the Khmer Rouge were tipping the patients out of the hospitals like garbage into the streets. Ban-daged men and women hobbled past the embassy, holding each other up. Wives pushed wounded soldier husbands down the street on wheeled hospital beds, some with serum drips and blood plasma bottles still attached. In five years of war, this was the greatest caravan of human misery I saw. The entire city was being emptied of its people: the old, the sick, the infirm, the hungry, the orphans, the little children, without exception. There were an estimated 20,000 wounded in Phnom Penh's hospitals at the end of the war. The Khmer Rouge must have known that few could survive the trek into the countryside; one could only conclude that they had no humanitarian instincts.

Murray Carmichael, the Scottish anaesthetist, said three-quarters of the medical team's work had been destroyed. Much of its time had been spent treating patients badly operated on, confined to bed, thin and wasting away. 'We taught them to walk again, put them on traction and got some unity into their bones. The Khmer Rouge told them to leave in ten minutes. These people have no compassion, no humanity. They are just here to do it their own way and it's nasty.' The team had performed only one operation under the new regime, saving a man who had been shot through the throat. 'Then we had to abandon him.'

It seemed that only the French embassy would remain, and for how long? Already about 1500 people were sheltering in it and more refugees were still jumping over the wall. We foreigners were relatively well-off having taken over the function room. The air-conditioning and water supply were still working, but the large and elegant compound outside was choked with hundreds of Cambodians, Vietnamese and Chinese, camping like gypsies on the grass, hungry and afraid. Many French families were living in cars which they had driven into the grounds; there were about one hundred of these makeshift homes. The spacious gardens of tamarinds and palms were black with people; smoke rose from scores of wood fires; the embassy was like one giant camp site. Dogs and children were everywhere. The embassy gates were now locked, but still crowds tried to enter.

Jean Dyrac, the French consul, had been on the radio to Paris all night seeking instructions. I have seldom seen so much anguish on a man's face as he constantly turned people away from the gates. A *tricolore* hanging limply from a pole spelt out the message that the embassy was sovereign French territory. But what did French sovereignty matter amidst this revolutionary mayhem and the dumb power of the gun?

Then the water in the compound ran out. Khmer Rouge soldiers were outside the gates demanding to come in. One man entered, dressed in black, shook hands with Dyrac and went inside the chancery. There was a lot of sporadic shooting in the city. The Khmer Rouge seemed to be using more ammunition than they did during the war. Soldiers drove up and down outside the embassy in half-tracks, peering through its walls. A US Phantom made two passes overhead, presumably on a photo-reconnaissance flight which we hoped would not provoke Khmer Rouge retaliation.

Each had his tale of terror to tell about the clearing of the city. The people in Adolphe Lesnik's building spent a hair-raising night hiding in the darkness from drunken soldiers who had invaded the car park and were playing with the cars like delinquent children, tooting horns, fiddling with the lights.

An hour before dawn, five black-clothed women forced their way in a frenzy into the building, firing into the air, and gave everyone ten minutes to get out. When the deadline expired, they fired another burst through the window and pointed their rifles at Lesnik's stomach. He understood and made for the door. One of the women snatched his watch and indicated she wanted the keys to all cars. 'It was all done by sign language, fingers and guns,' he said. In forty years in Asia, Lesnik, the director of an Anglo–French tobacco company, had been an unwilling witness to much human misery. In the 1930s he had seen the Japanese war in Manchuria. In World War Two he had been imprisoned in China. In 1947 he was in Shanghai when it fell to the communists. Now he said, 'This is enough. I'm going home to Montpellier.'

I still think of the hopelessness of those embassy days with sorrow and dread. I kept a diary, which is the basis of this account – a mixture of horror, absurdity, melodrama, human courage and betrayal. I wept when I wrote it and there are moments when I weep now. The people who were in that embassy will carry the pain to the end of their days; no words of mine can help their suffering.

For the next eleven days, we foreigners were confined to the grounds of the embassy. Our sole links with the outside world were the embassy radio and the BBC which we listened to breathlessly. It quoted a Sihanouk spokesman in Paris as giving assurances that members of the Lon Nol regime would be judged in a humanitarian way. By the time we heard that broadcast many of them had probably already been killed, no doubt brutally, begging for mercy.

Among the foreigners who had found refuge in the embassy were twenty-two journalists, fifteen members of the Red Cross, including the Scottish medical team, six United Nations officials and a handful of other nationalities, including Americans. The leader of these so-called 'internationals' was Paul Ignatieff, a tall distinguished-looking Canadian who was director of the UNICEF mission in Phnom Penh.

He came to report to us in our quarters that Dyrac had made

'pretty significant progress' during two meetings with the Khmer Rouge authorities who called themselves the Comité de la Ville.

'The Khmer Rouge he is dealing with are very intelligent, dedicated and serious people. We are a small problem to them and it is encouraging that they have taken time out to come and see us.' However, Friday, our first full day in captivity, ended with the looting still going on, bangs and machine-gun fire from the direction of the airport, and a fire in the west of the city; perhaps houses burning. Darkness came with us feeling bewildered and nervous.

On Saturday morning, Michael Daly decided he had to operate on a Cambodian soldier with an infected neck wound who had been smuggled into the compound. The Khmer Rouge refused him permission to use Calmette, the French hospital next door, the only one in the city still functioning under French medical staff unable to leave.

The operation was carried out in the embassy dining-room. Daly laid the soldier out on a sideboard covered with a linen tablecloth. He used surgical instruments off a silver tray. A lampstand became a drip support. Children peered through a window. Very delicately, he probed the man's wound. It did not look good. Halfway through, he shook his head at me. The man haemorrhaged. His life spurted onto the tablecloth and spread in a red pool over the floor. When he died, the room was stilled. Then his wife let out a shriek that cut through us like ice. Her tears mingled with his blood on the floor. A small burial party went out into the garden and dug a grave under the embassy wall. Michael took it particularly badly and blamed the Khmer Rouge for its refusal to let him collect blood transfusion equipment from the hospital next door.

*

In the afternoon we moved into the French ambassador's residence. The *salle de réception*, our old abode, was given over to the French staff of Calmette. They were being thrown out. Our new quarters were luxurious, littered with chandeliers, and sharp-eyed Ignatieff had liberated cases of Scotch and champagne from the cellar. For the first time since the city's fall, we relaxed a little, drinking while Martin Bloecher of the Asian Christian Service, a West German, played on the piano. The alcohol went through us with a rush. Food was scarce, and two bowls of rice were all I had eaten for two days. We estimated that the embassy probably contained more than a million dollars' worth of cash and gold smuggled in suitcases by the refugees. The Khmer Rouge had abolished money and reverted to the barter system. They had ransacked the banks. There was to be no place for money in the peasant revolution. But at least one was not averse to bribery. An Indian businessman said he had paid a black-clad guerrilla US$1000 not to execute him.

That evening, I stood near the front gate. A column of fresh troops marched into the city and refugees, crushed by fear, hurried the other way, their children giggling as they pushed trolleys of luggage down the road. For the uncomprehending young, it was a fun day. Big explosions rocked the city again. Plumes of smoke ringed it like funeral pyres. Then the staff of Calmette arrived with more accounts of Khmer Rouge cruelty and madness. For two days, they said, they had operated ceaselessly on communist wounded, looking down the barrels of guns.

'The Khmer Rouge threatened to kill me if I didn't save the life of one man,' said Bernard Piquart, a surgeon. Others had guns put to their heads and grenades dangled before their noses. Finally the

Khmer Rouge threw everyone out, after smashing in the medicine cupboards with their rifle butts.

All this time, hundreds of Cambodians were sheltering in the embassy; Pran was one of them. Since our arrival, we had managed to keep him safely with us as one of the 'internationals'. We had also found shelter for some of the Cambodian journalists, interpreters and their families. But most were having to camp outdoors on the grass.

I awoke the next morning to find the Scottish team playing bridge in the garden. There was the usual wisecrack about British phlegm in a tight spot. The banter did not last long. Word spread that the Khmer Rouge were reclassifying the embassy as an international regroupment centre for foreigners only. Implicit in its loss of diplomatic status was that it was no longer protected foreign territory and the Khmer Rouge soldiers could enter, without warning, at any time, and force the Cambodians out at gunpoint.

The bridge game broke up in silence as Dyrac came to tell the Cambodians they should leave in the interests of self-preservation. He had made these poor people who had jumped over the wall welcome from the beginning. But now he was afraid; if they remained, the victorious guerrillas might force their way in to eject them. There might be uncontrollable violence and bloodshed inside the grounds. A lot of the credit for keeping the Khmer Rouge out thus far was due to François Bizot, the French ethnologist, who had lived in Cambodia for eleven years. He used his fluent Khmer to act as a go-between with the Khmer Rouge authorities headquartered in the old South Korean embassy across the boulevard. He was also frequently at the front gate to defuse tension whenever a soldier tried to come in, which was two or three times a day. It was a desperate game. The embassy was defenceless. But Bizot was a master of the technique of bluff. He was one of that rare breed of men who thrive in adversity. His kidnapping by the Khmer Rouge four years before had given him first hand experience of their methods and how to handle them. The mother of Hélène, his daughter, had left Phnom Penh for the countryside like everyone else. But he was too big a man to speak of personal tragedy amid such universal suffering.

The news fell like a death sentence. Hundreds of Cambodians – as well as Vietnamese and Chinese who had lived their lives in Cambodia and regarded themselves as Cambodians – packed up a few belongings and prepared to leave. The odd thing was that so few of them expressed surprise at being ejected. They were numbed and resigned, and bleakly stared ahead. Here and there, some cried quietly. We shared our food with them and with heavy hearts watched them trudge towards the front gate – women, children, elderly people, friends. As they moved in a tattered column towards the Khmer Rouge soldiers waiting for them they did not look back – had they done so they would have seen many of us break down into tears. Suddenly it rained. It usually did at funerals.

The Khmer Rouge had split up whole families – French husbands could stay, but Cambodian wives and children had to go unless they had French papers. Many wives and children of Frenchmen did not have passports, either because they had never bothered to apply or because they had married in a Cambodian ceremony under Cambodian law. There were also many common-law wives. All these the Khmer Rouge regarded as Cambodians.

I turned round to find Doug Sapper, a decorated ex-Green Beret. 'You know, Jon, I have been a fighting man all my life,' he said. 'But I am not built for this kind of stuff. I haven't cried since I was ten years old.'

One Cambodian couple I knew gave away their seven-month-old baby which would never survive the long march into the countryside. I was too choked to look them in the face as they handed the boy to a Frenchwoman to be cared for. 'He is my only baby. He is a beautiful baby,' the wife sobbed, holding him in her arms for the last time and smothering his face with kisses of love and wet tears.

The French had already collected all our passports and at the Comité de la Ville's request were making lists of all the people in the embassy. We had to try to keep Pran with us. Sydney was insistent. Although his family was safely out of Cambodia, having been evacuated with the Americans, Pran had stayed to help Sydney cover the city's fall for the *New York Times*. Now it had all gone horribly wrong and Sydney felt overwhelming responsibility for his Cambodian assistant, reinforced by the fact that Pran, with his loyalty and quickness of mind, had saved all our lives.

We could think of only one solution: to forge a second British passport I had and give it to Pran as his own. Armed with this and a new identity, we imagined he could stay with us. That he looked Asian was not an insurmountable barrier, for he could perhaps pass himself off as a Nepalese holder of a British passport. There was a similarity of features. It was a chance but it might work.

There was no time to lose. Using a razor-blade, Al Rockoff scraped off my picture and replaced it with one of Pran. For glue, we used a gummy mixture of water and rice. More difficult was erasing my name. In the end we had to compromise: Pran became John Ancketill Brewer – my first three names. It was quite a mouthful to pronounce for a Briton, let alone a Cambodian turned Nepalese; he walked around the building repeating 'John Ancketill Brewer' until he was reasonably word perfect. Duly doctored, his British passport, number C352165, issued by the British embassy, Saigon, on 11 December 1973, was handed in to the consulate and we settled down to wait and hope.

A little while later, a group of solemn-faced embassy officials came to see us. Shaking their heads sadly, they gave back my passport, saying it was a good try but they had seen through the forgery immediately. They imagined the Khmer Rouge would too. What would Pran do in a confrontation? Would he be able to bluff it out? The next few hours were a nightmare as we agonised what to do. In the end Pran took the decision for us.

People were still leaving the city. We could see them toiling down the road outside, bedraggled and broken. But the numbers were dwindling. Pran decided the longer he was identified with foreigners in the embassy the tougher time he would have afterwards justifying himself to the Khmer Rouge. He would leave with the next batch of Cambodians who were even then packing their things in preparation for departure and try to make it across the border to Thailand.

We said goodbye to Pran, with whom we had shared the bitterest and most frightening minutes of our lives. Sydney gave him a lot of money, several thousand dollars. We gave him the rest of our food. He wore his *chroma* over his shoulders. There was a profound silence. There were tears. He joined the other Cambodians at the embassy

155

gates. The gates swung back and Pran and the other Cambodians passed through, holding each other, trying to be brave, their belongings in the back of a Toyota pickup which they started to push down the road.

He had taught us what friendship meant and when his luck ran out we had nothing to give him except money and food. Our abandonment of him confirmed in me the belief that we journalists were in the end just privileged passengers in transit through Cambodia's landscape of hell. We were eyewitnesses to a great human tragedy none of us could comprehend. We had betrayed our Cambodian friends. We had been unable to save those who had saved us. We were protected simply because our skins were white. I felt ashamed.

All this time, Prince Sirik Matak was a fugitive in the embassy. Ever since the day of Phnom Penh's fall and his request for political asylum, he had been hiding in a tiny storeroom beneath the stairs in the consulate building. The French had told him to keep the door locked and to open it only to a coded series of knocks. The Khmer Rouge had condemned Matak to death as one of the 'arch traitors'. Harbouring him was a huge risk, but Dyrac believed it was his duty as consul to protect the prince and a Cambodian general who had sought asylum at the same time. Dyrac rather naïvely counted on being able to keep the two men secret from the Khmer Rouge. But they now told him to hand over the prince and the general or they would come in and drag them out at gunpoint.

With a heavy heart, Dyrac, accompanied by Bizot, went to the storeroom and knocked on the door in code. It opened and at once the two men were overcome by a stench of human faeces. The prince had been cooped up inside this airless chamber for three days. Unable to leave, he had used a drawer as a lavatory.

He was stripped down to a singlet and shorts. Bizot explained the situation; Dyrac was too overcome to speak. At once, the prince stood up, threw open an attaché case on the desk before him, looked the Frenchmen in the eye and said, 'I know what I must do.' Bizot was afraid the prince was reaching for a pistol to shoot himself. Instinctively, he turned the key in the door, 'Don't do that,' he said. But the prince took out only a beige T-shirt and a pair of trousers, which he slipped on without another word. Then, with great dignity, he said to the two Frenchmen, 'I am ready now.'

So Prince Sirik Matak walked out of the embassy and into the hands of the Khmer Rouge. He knew he was walking out to die. He was old and thin. But he walked erect, upright and strong like a proud tree. His lips were set firm, and as he passed the threshold he turned to Migot, a Frenchman guarding the gate, shook his hand, and said with a touching calmness, 'I am not afraid. I am ready to explain and to give account of what I have done.' The Khmer Rouge had come for him with rifles in an army lorry drawn up outside the gate. They looked at him with curiosity, but not evilly. The engine was throbbing and the rain was falling steadily. He got in and was driven away. The general, by contrast, a roly-poly man, was escorted out quaking with fear. 'It's very sad, but what else could we do?' said Dyrac, who turned the prince out so as not to compromise our chances of survival. 'Nous ne sommes plus les hommes' – and I saw that Dyrac, who had been a prisoner of the Germans, and knew what it was like to suffer, was weeping and his face was dead white.

No one knows the precise details of Sirik Matak's fate and the

157

Khmer Rouge are not telling. But that he died horribly is almost certain. It is reported that he was taken to a stadium about half a mile away and killed there along with other high-ranking officials of the Lon Nol regime.

That night, Jean-Jacques Cazaux married his Cambodian girlfriend, Thani Pho, to give her French nationality in the hope of saving her skin. The consul backdated the marriage to 12 April, to trick the Khmer Rouge. I shall never understand why there were not many more such weddings, for there were plenty of French passports in the embassy. Our hearts were heavy. But we fêted the wedding with embassy champagne and a Dundee cake.

Outside, the atmosphere was sinister. Headlamps ablaze, trucks of soldiers went up and down, searching for people hiding in the city. Gunfire crashed in the suburbs. We were witnesses perhaps to the deaths of thousands; the destruction of a way of life.

In the morning, the 150 Montagnards also had to leave the compound. These hill people had fought for the Americans in Vietnam and Cambodia for ten years and this was the end of the road. They shouldered their pots and pans and buried their money and valuables. They harboured no illusions about the fate awaiting them.

A mother screamed over the four-day-old baby she had to leave behind. She pressed jewellery into our hands and clasped us for comfort. Tears were running down our cheeks.

It was not a lack of bravery that had beaten them. They were a lost people. A Frenchwoman sobbed over her five children and the

Montagnard husband she could not follow. 'My babies, my babies,' she cried.

Ragged, but proud, the Montagnards moved out.

Now Khmer Rouge soldiers with guns moved in and searched the compound, as we had feared. They looked and poked and did not smile. They called all remaining Asians to check their nationalities and told them they, too, had to leave. Then they changed their minds, playing on our tattered nerves.

Dyrac had raised the question of urgent evacuation with Paris. An intensely humble and decent man, he was often at loggerheads with some of the hard-headed French *colons* who had lost all their worldly possessions in Cambodia and despised his ponderous style. We owed him much.

There were also those with whom we, who had abandoned our Cambodian friends, did not wish to pass the time of day. One was Shane Tarr, a twenty-four-year-old New Zealander and his Cambodian wife (who, if she was lucky, would be able to stay). He was full of self-righteous and nauseating revolutionary rhetoric and extolled the deeds of the 'liberation forces'. That the Khmer Rouge had kicked two million people out into the countryside without making adequate provision to feed them; looted the city; ripped off watches, radios, cars; and executed people, did not trouble his conscience. 'They are not looting. They are expropriating private property,' he said. 'The people give up their things willingly.'

But when it came down to it he was as bourgeois and in need of creature comforts as the rest of us. Nearly always first in line for the food which we ate at 3p.m. – a soggy mixture of rice sprinkled with fragments of meat or vegetable – he complained bitterly when the air-conditioning stopped. And he did little work. He and his wife,

Chou Meng, fraternised with the Khmer Rouge guards over the walls. The more paranoid among us worried they might be passing on our little secrets. He had a low opinion of the capitalist press; as we had of his hypocrisy. He was shunned.

With no end to our internment in sight, the shortage of food was becoming serious. Reluctantly, Jean Menta, a Corsican adventurer, and Borella, the mercenary who had been keeping a low profile in case he was recognised, strangled and skinned the embassy cat. The poor creature put up a spirited fight and both men were badly scratched. A few of us ate it, curried. The meat was tender like chicken. It was clear that after a few more weeks of this we would be real savages. (We already were as far as one cat-loving woman from Yorkshire was concerned, for in that queer English way that sometimes puts animals before human beings she wrote a letter afterwards in which she condemned me as a 'murderer', and completely ignored the sufferings of the Cambodian people.)

The next day life suddenly got easier. The Khmer Rouge seemed to be loosening up. Presumably this was because the Cambodians we were harbouring had left. They brought us water from the Mekong and several pigs in the back of a lorry. Sapper killed the first, knocking it out with a neat axe-blow, then slitting its throat with his jungle knife. Daly, the surgeon, used his surgical skills to clean it. There were eighty-two kilos of meat for more than 600 people remaining in the grounds.

But tempers were fraying. The squabbling over food was fantastic. Some people had a lot; some almost none. The officials in the chancery were eating turkey, and at one point, I saw a Frenchman toss a steak to his dog. The Calmette doctors had a sideboard stacked

160

with food and booze which they refused to share. We labelled them
petits Français and they hated us for it. I remember Albert Spaccessi,
patron of the Café de Paris. He had cooked for Général de Gaulle
on his controversial 1966 visit to Phnom Penh (when the general
delivered an inflammatory speech about the neutrality of Indo-China
which outraged the United States). Now Spaccessi was lamenting
that he had recently re-equipped his restaurant with a chic new
dinner service for one hundred place settings. 'What will become of
it?' he moaned. Poor Spaccessi, his outsize tummy carried an enormous scar from an operation to cut out kilos of excess fat. He was
feeling very lost indeed. I often wondered what became of him and
learned later that he ran a restaurant in Marseilles where he died of
diabetes.

There was increasing danger of disease. We had dug latrines in
the grounds. But there were already more than one hundred cases
of diarrhoea. Non-existent sanitation had turned the compound into
a disagreeable collection of faeces. Dr Henri Revil, the médecin-chef
of Calmette, was constantly cabling Paris about the growing health
problem. There was already a case of hepatitis. As there was no
water, we collected the drips from the air-conditioners and drank
those. And when it rained, we stripped off and washed. I remember
a particularly heavy downpour when, with one accord, we rushed
outside, threw off our clothes and stood naked in the rain. Bizot ran
naked through the grounds, with Avi, his boxer dog, barking and
gambolling at his side. It was a refreshing and spontaneous act that
eased the tension. We gave him a thunderous round of applause but
he told me later that some of the French had complained about his
frivolité.

It was gratifying also to find that Khmer Rouge xenophobia

encompassed even comrades from the socialist countries of Eastern Europe. They expelled Herr Stange, the East German diplomat. I watched him climb down from his white embassy van loaded with embassy furniture he hoped to take with him. The French ordered him to leave it outside. He was dishevelled and very angry. He had been on the last flight into Cambodia with me before the city's fall, and I had found his enthusiasm for the imminent Khmer Rouge victory and the humbling of America nauseating. Now he ran over and grasped my hand. 'I never expected this. We must have been mad to come back,' he said. 'How can they do this to me?' Stange had several times refused to quit his embassy. 'But today,' he said, 'a Khmer Rouge with four pencils in his breast pocket – a colonel, I know these things by now – was very firm, and gave us two hours to get out. I told him he knew very well that for five years East Germany had recognised his government, but he just shrugged. I understand. He is a peasant and behind him is another one. There is no use to argue with such people.'

Stange was billeted with us. When he saw our overcrowded room, he was so downcast it was funny. We introduced him to Martin Bloecher, his West German 'countryman'. We told him this was a workers' camp and he could work in the kitchen, sweep, dig latrines. He was not amused. But that night he became more affable and chattered away with Bloecher while the whisky flowed and some of us smoked grass.

There was a stir at the front gate. Jean-Pierre Martini, my French Maoist friend, arrived with Danielle, his pretty wife, after five voluntary days with Khmer Rouge forces in the countryside. True believers, when the city fell they had donned black pyjamas and Ho Chi Minh sandals and joined the mass exodus from the city. About ten miles out, they were stopped at a Khmer Rouge roadblock and sent back. Now they wanted sanctuary at the embassy. As the doors swung open, Migot, the Frenchman guarding the gate, saw them in Khmer Rouge uniform and exploded with rage. He walked up to Jean-Pierre and slapped him hard on the face with a crack like a gunshot. 'Enlevez-moi ça,' he shouted. The pair of them were forced to strip off their black pyjamas on the spot and put on western clothes.

I could not get much sense out of Jean-Pierre as he was so awestruck by developments. But he assured us as he lit up his usual joint, that the Khmer Rouge smoked grass too. He said they had sealed off each section of the city for searching. They did not take risks, but fired grenades and B40 rockets into buildings where snipers might still be hiding. If they could not search a building or street efficiently, they burned it down with incendiary grenades, he said.

Our forced confinement continued for another eight days. There were more times of tension – one when Khmer Rouge soldiers accompanied by French officials carried out a spot check of all our belongings. They claimed there was a spy in the compound with a secret radio transmitter. But a search of photographer Denis Cameron's bags revealed a surprise: a bundle of French embassy silverware – coffee pots and bowls – tumbled onto the floor. He had taken them as souvenirs. The French were incandescent with rage. 'People are dying while you are lining your pockets,' Dyrac screamed. It was wrong. But Denis's justification was that the silver would be left behind anyway when the embassy was finally abandoned; it was better he should have it than the Khmer Rouge. Cameron had stayed behind to try to arrange the evacuation of 500 orphans to Australia.

For much of the time, he sat morosely in his corner, obsessively killing flies with a spray. The spray choked Rockoff's lungs and sent him into coughing fits, but he could not dissuade Cameron. Rockoff's heart had stopped when he had been seriously wounded the year before, and he owed his life to prompt surgery by a Swedish Red Cross team. 'You are going to die,' we joked as he spluttered and coughed. 'It won't be the first time,' Rockoff said.

On Wednesday, 30 April, a first convoy carrying about 600 foreigners left for the Thai border. The Khmer Rouge announced the evacuation plan at the end of a three-day special national congress. The French had offered to provide transport planes, but the Khmer Rouge refused. The congress also said Cambodia's new rulers would countenance no foreign interference, either military or humanitarian – sad news indeed for the many tens of thousands they had forced at gunpoint into the countryside, who had been dependent on international relief agencies for several years and who needed it all now more than ever.

Our last day was especially trying. The Khmer Rouge once more showed an amazing ability to turn nasty, suddenly announcing that no Asian without papers could leave. This meant splitting up more families. There were tearful, emotional scenes. Fear, apprehension, panic were once more written on people's faces. And when, at 4 a.m., we were told to line up to board Khmer Rouge lorries, several of us wondered if we would ever reach Thailand.

Our departure was chaotic. A fleet of twenty-six open army lorries had drawn up outside the embassy. We were crammed in, twenty-four to a lorry, with our belongings. In the crush, Bizot managed to smuggle aboard two or three Cambodian women who had still been sheltering in the embassy. Among them was the wife of Tarr, the revolutionary New Zealander. At the last minute, Bizot, ingenious as ever, pushed the weeping couple into a truck behind the backs of the guards. Perhaps they had now a taste of what revolution was all about. The awful realisation sunk in that had Pran still been with us we could probably have smuggled him out the same way. But how could we have known?

The convoy left Phnom Penh on a circuitous route that avoided Highway Five, the main axis of the population's exodus. Five years before, Phnom Penh had been one of the loveliest cities in Southeast Asia. It was not only the old French colonial architecture, the glittering pagodas, its romantic position beside the Mekong, that gave it its enchantment. It was the warmth and grace of its people even under siege. Now the people had gone and Phnom Penh, as we drove through the suburbs, was a sinister wasteland. Every single building in the city seemed to have been turned upside down in the soldiers' search for food and booty – from the Soviet embassy, where they stamped on President Leonid Brezhnev's picture and fired a B40 rocket through the window, to the stilted houses of the poor on the outskirts. They had wrecked the water plant and shut down the factories.

The empty, dustblown streets were lined with hundreds of abandoned cars and motor bikes, cannibalised by the Khmer Rouge, their tyres cut up to make Ho Chi Minh sandals. We passed whole districts gutted by fire, with hungry pigs and dogs rooting through the ruins for scraps.

The Khmer Rouge army, now the city's only occupants, showed little pride in its prize. The main attraction to these country boys who had fought and won a ferocious war against a corrupt US-backed regime, was the multitude of watches, radios and trinkets they had been able to loot from its shops. The road out of the city, past the airport, was littered with evidence of the hurried migration – a giant boneyard of everything from trucks and cars to helmets, uniforms and TV sets. The rotting vehicles were scattered for miles around, abandoned as the petrol ran out. Some drivers, angry at the thought of leaving what was probably their pride and joy to the Khmer Rouge, had pushed them into pools of stagnant water. Motorised transport in Cambodia was now almost non-existent. We were to see no more than half a dozen moving vehicles in our 260 mile journey to the frontier. They were driven by Khmer Rouge officers, and badly at that.

My mind groped and fumbled to explain the horror and enormity of Phnom Penh's emptying. There had been no 'bloodbath' in the conventional sense. But what was taking place was equally horrific. My overriding impression was that the Khmer Rouge had ordered this mass evacuation not to 'punish' the people but to 'revolutionise' their ways and thoughts. Many thousands would die. At the time, I was reluctant to conclude it was a deliberate campaign of terror. I thought it pointed rather to poor organisation, lack of vision and the brutalisation of a people by a long and savage war. I now know otherwise.

It took two bone-jarring days to traverse the first eighty miles from Phnom Penh because of the appalling condition of the roads and the lack of organisation by our guides. We lost our way and had to backtrack. Our frustration grew as we passed the same spot we had passed twelve hours before. Then two trucks broke down and, after yet another long delay, we were able to get moving again only by towing one of them. Much of our progress over the bomb-damaged roads was at less than five miles per hour.

We had come to an even more startling realisation: outside Phnom Penh, virtually every other city, town, village and hamlet that had resisted the communists had also been evacuated into the countryside. The greater part of this nation of seven million, which had endured òne of the most savage, futile wars of modern times, had been uprooted, its people hungry and bewildered and on the move.

That night, we reached the provincial capital of Kompong Chhnang and found it emptied of its 500,000 people. In the nearby countryside there was an opportunity to say a few fleeting words to a poor male nurse, Tong San, from Kompong Chhnang hospital. (He was recognised by the Scottish Red Cross team who had trained him.) He said that on 20 April Khmer Rouge soldiers had carried away all the hospital patients in lorries and dumped them eighteen miles inside the forest without food or water. For ten days now, Tong San had been wandering aimlessly. The Khmer Rouge had given nobody firm instructions as to where to go or what to do. They simply told them to keep moving. 'We are lost and confused,' he said. 'The Khmer Rouge do not accept money, so I exchange my clothes for rice to eat.'

We met Tong San in a long-established Khmer Rouge collective a few miles outside Kompong Chhnang. The villagers were a dull, uninspiring lot. Everyone wore black, and the women had Maoist pudding bowl haircuts. One of the marvellous things about Cambodia used to be the spontaneity and gaiety of its people, even towards strangers. Now a wave and a smile was met with wooden stares.

167

The war damage here, as everywhere else we saw, was total. Not a bridge, it seemed, was standing, hardly a house. I was told most of these villagers had spent the war years living semi-permanently in earth bunkers underground to escape the bombing. Little wonder that this peasant army was proud of its achievements. Sitting down with me to a meal of boiled rice and meat from a freshly killed pig, the local chief said: 'I and my men worked in fields during the day and fought at night. That is how we won.'

The entire countryside had been churned up by B52 bomb craters, whole towns and villages razed. So far, I had not seen one intact pagoda. At one particular village, where part of a 500lb American bomb hung from a tree as an air-raid signalling gong, we made a sordid spectacle of ourselves. Stampeding for food, breaking plates, tipping over bowls of rice and stealing coconuts in our haste to eat. Our wild behaviour surely hardened the Khmer Rouge's conviction that westerners had no business in their new society and were better out of Cambodia altogether.

Throughout this journey, some of the greediest, most selfish, among us were the Soviet diplomats and their wives. While the rest of us nibbled on a Red Cross biscuit and a handful of rice, they settled down in the evening to a four-course meal brought along with their personal possessions, washed down with vodka and tea. They also had the gall to demand their portion of the communal food. Nor did they share their meals with a Bulgarian woman in the same lorry, claiming she was our responsibility.

As the chorus of protests rose, the Russians threatened to expose those westerners who, with the connivance of Bizot, had smuggled Cambodian women aboard. Only when the journalists threatened to splash their names in the world's press and expose their bourgeois tastes and their refusal to feed one of their Warsaw Pact allies did they submit. We were delighted to receive a placatory bottle of vodka.

The night of Thursday, 1 May, was the lowest point of the journey. While our guides tried to find us somewhere to sleep, we sat for four hours in the open lorries in a driving rainstorm. We slept finally, wet through, on the stone floor of the magistrates' court in Kompong Chhnang. During the night a nine-month-old French baby died of exposure and exhaustion. She was wrapped in a sarong and buried at once. But by that time I had run out of tears. And my thoughts increasingly were focusing elsewhere for, listening to the BBC World Service that night, I heard that Saigon had fallen the previous day as our convoy bucked and bounced its way through the tormented Cambodian countryside. I tried to imagine the scene – the communist tanks bursting triumphantly through the gates of the presidential palace, the North Vietnamese soldiers padding down Tu Do street, peasant-victors in the big city. I knew that Jacqueline would be suffering. There was nothing I could do about it. She was very far away. I cursed my decision to come back to Cambodia on that last flight into beleagured Phnom Penh and wished I was with her in Saigon.

The journey was almost over. There was one last ugly incident as we approached Pursat. Our convoy was stopped by a group of Khmer Rouge soldiers who demanded that we hand over any Americans on board. We managed to bluff it out. Otherwise, the knots of Khmer Rouge soldiers we passed showed little interest in our presence.

In peacetime it used to take ten hours to drive the 260 miles from Phnom Penh to the Thai border. Our journey took four days. The Khmer Rouge drivers brought the trucks up to the bridge over a stream which marks the frontier. We tramped across it, unshaven, our clothes thick with sweat-caked dust. We were greeted on the other side by Thai officials, French diplomats, foreign journalists, Red Cross nurses offering sandwiches and orangeade. They had been waiting for the best part of a week for our arrival.

As I travelled down to Bangkok I reflected on the Cambodia we had left behind. In five years it had lost upwards of half a million people, nearly ten per cent of its population, in a war fuelled and waged on its soil by outside powers for their own selfish reasons. It was a wilderness of destruction. But I knew that if I thought too long about it that day, I would go mad with pity; and as the peaceful Thai countryside flashed by I longed to sink into the comfort of forgetfulness.

Hanoi

On the days
there is no mail from you
I sit quietly
in my room and reread
what I have . . .
because I love you
I am alone
for the first time
in my life . . .

For weeks I felt empty, overweighed by a sense of weariness and lost happiness. An epoch had ended in Indo-China. That much I knew, and I needed time to be alone, to think. My life was changed for ever. My sorrow at leaving Cambodia and Vietnam was deepened by the knowledge that I might never return. I was tormented by the beloved and poignant face of Jacqueline, whom I had deserted in Saigon at her darkest hour and from whom there was now only a ghostly silence.

But there was little time for brooding. The days flew breathlessly by. I had to be patient, and writing helped. I wrote the story of the fall of Phnom Penh for the *Sunday Times* and was invited to join the staff on the strength of it. The newspaper recognised that I had no desire to work in London; it was agreed I should base myself in Bangkok. I soon found myself a little Thai-style house near Samsen railway station on the main line to Chiang Mai and the north of Thailand. There I tried to begin life anew.

In those days, Bangkok was an agreeable place – not so much pollution, not so many roaring Hondas and cars clogging its streets, a softer, less brash nightlife. It was full of comrades – 'old Indo-China hands' – rootless souls like myself searching for a new beginning and a definition to life after our *raison d'être* had been torn away. We met each Saturday for a buffet lunch at the Foreign Correspondents' Club in an old wing, long since pulled down, of the Oriental Hotel; talked over old times and drowned our sorrows in beer and red wine. Spooks and diplomats on the fringes of the press corps liked to live vicariously through our outrageous stories of sexual adventures and derring-do, but they were outsiders; our stories and our laughter were really for our own benefit: the tightknit community linked by the common bond of comradeship and the hopeless courage of Indo-China. Our outward joviality and lack of moderation covered up, if we were honest, our sense of melancholia and gloom. Life seemed pointless. Nostalgia for Indo-China gnawed at our hearts; at least, it did at mine. The French call it *Le Mal Jaune*.

There would, no doubt, be other stories, other wars. Journalists who covered Indo-China were resilient if nothing else and in due course some drifted off to Lebanon and Angola, which were just heating up, in search of other wars to make them feel alive. I was convinced that for me there would never be another Indo-China, where everything had fused magically together as one perfect piece: the place, the war, the story, the woman I loved; making it the happiest and most romantic of places to be for a young man still flush with the optimism and raw idealism of youth.

My mood was melancholy. I was burnt-out, filled with weariness, a sense of unworthiness. No matter how much I tried to justify my actions I felt guilt of egotism and desertion. My journalistic life had been a success. I had quarried a rich harvest of stories out of Indo-China, the best of my life. But at what a disillusioning price.

I had been assured by colleagues who covered the defeat of Saigon and finally emerged from Vietnam that Jacqueline and her mother were safe and were trying to leave, together with many other Saigonese. I wrote to her, hoping for an answering letter that never came. Perhaps the mail was held up. Then late one afternoon, some weeks after the fall of Saigon, I got a call from a colleague to come to the Trocadero Hotel immediately. A surprise was waiting.

I arrived in trembling haste, not daring to guess what the surprise might be, but sensing inwardly that Jacqueline and her mother would be there. Sure enough, they were standing in the lobby. Wearily, they told me that they had planned to stay on in Saigon, having nowhere else to go and hoping life would settle down. But in a matter of days they had changed their minds. As the communists' grip on the city tightened and a dour authoritarianism prevailed, it became apparent that there was no future for them there. The communist rulers regarded them as being on the losing side and treated them, and many others like them, as conquered people. With a heavy heart, Jacqueline's mother gave her house over to her neighbour for safekeeping, and she and Jacqueline embarked on the heartbreaking task of getting their papers in order, so that they could leave Vietnam for ever. Obtaining an exit visa was a nightmare of red tape and obfuscation, despite their French nationality. Dominique, the *patron* of the Valinco, summed it all up in an outburst of frustration one day: 'Si les Vietcongs donnaient les visas de sortie, même les rats s'en iraient,' he declared.

It took Dominique well over a year to leave Saigon, and Jacqueline and her mother almost half as long. The only residents who seemed to have prospered from the 'liberation' were some foreign journalists who had stayed behind in Saigon. Not only did they have the satisfaction of covering a momentous event; they took over Saigon's

British Club and liberated its booze and patriotically saved the abandoned British embassy's Union Jack which they found had been torn down from the flagpole and was now a canopy over a squatter's shack.

Jacqueline and her mother left Saigon for ever, their possessions stuffed into a couple of trunks, all the French would allow on the evacuation flight. Because they had left Vietnam of their own accord, the French government later denied them compensation for the house and belongings that they had lost. But not a word of complaint at its injustice passed their lips. Like the people of Vietnam they had grown accustomed to battling their way through life and accepted their loss with stoic, quiet suffering.

Now the anguish of the past weeks was swept away. Jacqueline's mother soon left for Paris and Jacqueline and I remained for a while in the little house by the railway station with its garden of hibiscus, palms and frangipani, its whirling ceiling fans and croaking frogs.

At four each morning, the house reverberated as the express from Chiang Mai thundered past. But nothing could disturb us as we snuggled together, intoxicated at being lovers once more.

There were high moments. We travelled together to Burma, where an earthquake had done terrible damage to many of the 5000 temples of the ancient city of Pagan, the former capital. There we met Major Dick Bone, one of the most extraordinary British characters in Asia.

Dick Bone's romantic story was in the tradition of a Somerset Maugham novel. On St Valentine's Day 1945, as a young lieutenant in the Fourteenth Army, he had taken part in the capture of Pagan from the Japanese. Clambering up the cliffs of the east bank of the Irrawaddy, he found himself surrounded by dark forms rising through the dawn mist – the ruins of hundreds of temples dotting

176

the Pagan plain. This awe-inspiring sight affected him deeply. He went on to Rangoon and fell in love with a Burmese woman Thein Wa, to the disapproval of his race-conscious superior officers; once the war was over, they transferred him to Singapore under a cloud. Before leaving, Bone gave her rubies as a token of his love, with the assurance he would come back to her. True to his word, he resigned his commission and smuggled himself back to Burma on an RAF freight plane, registering himself on the flight manifest as 'bones'.

Bone never left Burma again. He stayed on through all that sad and beautiful country's troubles, a brave spirit, often in penury, often unwell. When his little bookshop in Rangoon was nationalised overnight by the Ne Win government pursuing its imbecile 'Burmese way to Socialism', he worked as a navvy on the roads to make ends meet. This was too much for the status-conscious British embassy; to its eternal shame, the embassy struck him off its invitation list to the Queen's birthday party as unsuitable. Bone contemptuously handed in his British passport and took Burmese nationality.

I think he and Thein Wa were as humanly happy as it was possible to be. But Bone's first love was always Pagan. Whenever he had money to spare, which was not often, he would spend it on an expedition to the temples, sometimes staying for weeks. He became one of the greatest living experts on this venerated spot, with a library of thousands of photographs and countless learned essays.

He deserved to die with Pagan engraved on his heart for he was faithful to it even in death. A few months after we saw him, he was being driven from Rangoon to the temples in the French ambassador's car on one of the narrow Burmese roads. A lorry smashed into them and both men were killed. A 'Burmese born in

177

England' was how his Burmese friends described him; an exceptional tribute.

Bone and Thein Wa were excessively kind to Jacqueline and me. They were inspiring in their love and respect for the values of Asia. Thinking of Burma always reminds me of Bone and the serenity and peace of our visit to Pagan. I can see him now at sunset, the hour of the day he loved best, his elfin figure sitting in the cool of the evening on the terrace of the Thatpinyu, a Burmese cheroot sparking in his hand, his soft benevolent eyes watching the sun drop below the horizon, his extraordinary life going by.

In Bangkok, Jacqueline and I talked of the future but I do not think I recognised adequately how her optimism had been blunted by the disillusionment of her flight. The idea of living in Europe, even France, the country of her birth, dismayed her; she knew she would be out of place under those northern skies, the damp winter cold; everything was overshadowed by the crushing loss of her Saigon.

'Mon Indo-Chine est morte,' she said with heartrending finality one day and I understood exactly what she meant. Indo-China was her anchorage. All that she valued in life was linked to it and now she had said goodbye for ever to the world she had always known. How little outsiders grasped the humiliation and demoralising sense of her loss. Walking down Tu Do street a few days after the communist capture of the city, she had encountered one of my colleagues who, throwing his arms around her and planting a kiss on her cheeks, said thoughtlessly, 'What on earth are you looking so unhappy for, *ma belle*? Why, Saigon is *la dolce vita* now.' She was too gripped by sorrow to explain that for many ordinary Saigonese this was the unhappiest time of their lives.

I hoped my presence lightened some of her misery; I am not sure. There was an impotence of spirit. A crisis in our relationship was looming. Cambodia lay between us like an open wound and with a sinking heart I realised it was impossible to live again our past in Saigon, or to wash away my sense of failure at having abandoned her. There was a moment when we could have stayed together. I think I neglected it through irresolution as I grappled with the circumstances of a new life. So, in due course, Jacqueline flew to Paris to join her mother, while I carried on in Thailand as best I could. It was very hard saying goodbye. We intended it to be a short separation; it continued, as these things do, for several barren months.

There was plenty to write about, to keep my mind from plunging into despair. Several times I went to stay with Dr Chester Gorman, the brilliant American archaeologist, at his base in northeast Thailand. In two years of excavations of burial mounds at Ban Chiang left by prehistoric man, Chet had turned up a wealth of early bronze Age artefacts dating back to 3500 BC. In the light of his findings, scholars suggested that the Bronze Age might have dawned in Southeast Asia. Chet taught me that 6000 years ago this depressed area of northeast Thailand bordering on the Mekong had been one of the most advanced in the world, inhabited by people who had mastered the techniques of metallurgy and rice agriculture. Chet died, alas, prematurely from cancer a few years later. His scholarship remains.

Soon afterwards I went to Vientiane, the charming and sleepy capital of Laos on the banks of the Mekong. The defeat of America here had not been as brutal or abrupt as in Cambodia and Vietnam. People said that gentleness had traditionally been the Lao way and it was to some degree true. Nevertheless, since May, when the communist Pathet Lao had begun to take control of the country, a good quarter of the city's 180,000 inhabitants had fled; not just corrupt politicians, but doctors and qualified people, and those with much to lose. I found myself badgered by bewildered people wondering what to do. Typical was my driver, who had gone home one night to find his brother and sister had swum the Mekong to Thailand. In a town full of informers, they bolted without telling him.

The French community had made Laos the last white enclave in communist Indo-China. They called it 'Le Pays de Cocagne' – a Provençal expression standing for 'the country of milk and honey'. Now many of them, too, were going, abandoning their homes in the face of the communist take-over. One I knew made a dramatic escape in a stolen light plane which he flew across the Mekong and landed on a main road in Thailand. The departure of the French who ran so much of Vientiane's commerce had led to the town falling into elegant decay. Many shops had closed. Others, deprived of custom, were selling wares *en masse*. And what wares they were: champagne and fine French wine at less than a pound a bottle, furniture, silver, antiques, all going for a song. At the French Mission Militaire, a quaint hangover from the 1954 Geneva Accords, a horse belonging to the riding school was for sale for a fiver.

Laos's new rulers, the communist Pathet Lao, out to create a new society unsullied by western influences, were glad to see the back of the French, many of whom were *colons*, army veterans and gangsters who stayed behind after the French military withdrawal in 1954. At seminars and meetings, in songs and slogans, the communists drummed it into the people that the western ideas which had dominated their lives for so long were evil. They taught them to be proud of the Lao language, its culture and traditions. This emphasis on the old Lao values had a sobering impact on what had been one of the seedier towns in Southeast Asia. Crime and prostitution, once rampant, had largely been eliminated in just a few months. Thieves were paraded through the streets with placards around their necks denouncing their crimes, then sent into the countryside for reeducation. The Pathet Lao claimed they had achieved these reforms without bloodshed. They abolished the 600-year-old monarchy, banishing the king and his family to a re-education camp. But they still allowed the king's portrait to hang on the walls of private houses.

I had spent some time in Laos in 1971 and had liked the seedy charm and wackiness of Vientiane. The country had known war for a quarter of a century; yet there was no sense of urgency. Here there was Madame Lulu's, famous for 'oral sex and warm beer'. There was the White Rose, the most famous whorehouse in Vientiane, where Trevor Wilson, the local head of MI6, reputedly typed his secret dispatches for London while sitting on the steps, a girl on one side, his deputy on the other. There was the Purple Porpoise bar, on the shore of the Mekong, run by an Englishman, filled with hard pilots of Air America, the CIA airline. There were some fine French restaurants. Vientiane was also full of French *minables* and *charlots*.

Typical were the three Corsicans who decided they would rob the Banque de l'Indochine on Friday when the accumulated money was flown to Bangkok for protection. They were puzzling how to get

181

through Vientiane airport security onto the tarmac to grab the sacks of money as they were delivered to the aircraft, when one of them had a brainwave; the bishop of Vientiane's private chauffeur could be their driver. The robbery went ahead without a mishap. The bishop's car had an airport pass; security waved it through with a flourish. Stocking-masked and throwing copious quantities of pepper, the crooks jumped out, overwhelmed the bank guards and grabbed the money. Vientiane was in uproar; there had never been such an audacious robbery. But it ended in tears. Conscience-stricken by what he had done, the chauffeur confessed to the bishop later that same day; disregarding the secrecy of the confessional, the bishop tipped off the police. By midnight, two of the crooks had been arrested. The third was picked up the next morning; he had had the gumption to escape across the Mekong to Thailand with his share and was driving into Bangkok when his car suffered a puncture in front of Bangkok airport. A friendly policeman strolled over to help, opened the boot and found it filled with the stolen money. All three were behind bars within twenty-four hours, hardly the Napoleons of crime they had dreamed of being.

The British had their characters, too, chief among whom perhaps was Ed Fillingham, who worked for the World Bank and whose job was to balance the Lao *kip*, the local currency. He did so each week with a briefcase of dollars, the Lao economy was so small. 'Sacré Ed,' his French friends called him, and with good reason, for Fillingham was a drinker who earned his nickname 'Filling Station'. He had a delightful mischievous streak, which sometimes landed him in trouble. His French friends told me that he disgraced himself one year at an evening party in the garden of the British ambassador's residence; I think it was the Queen's birthday party. Ed mysteriously turned up with two tall stone jars which, with a nudge and a wink, he placed in the garden among the guests who were by now quite used to his pranks. This was a party trick to savour. Out popped two naked beauties, who darted through the grounds illuminated by the fairy-lights. Ed had hired them for the night from the White Rose to be served up naked at the embassy party. The ambassador may have been amused; his wife was not.

Vientiane seemed to attract the most eccentric of British diplomats. John Lloyd was a profoundly left-wing and anti-American ambassador who talked openly about the 'Americans and their beastly bombers', to the embarrassment of his staff. Alan Davidson, his successor, was more discreet. He arrived to take up his post on the day of one of Vientiane's periodic coups. His big passion was fish, and he later became the author of several authoritative books on seafood. He carried his secret papers about in an old fishing bag, and his secretary once complained that he had turned the embassy into a fishery research station; the fridge was full of fishy specimens from the Mekong. On one occasion, hearing of the capture of a giant Mekong catfish in the upper reaches of the river, Davidson dropped everything, flew to the site in the north of Laos, bought the fish's huge head from the fishermen and took it back to the embassy. The catfish is one of Asia's rarest fishes, in danger of extinction. I think today Davidson's specimen is in the Natural History Museum in London.

In October I went to Hanoi, the wartime capital of North Vietnam. I passed myself off as a schoolteacher, hiding the fact that I had been a journalist in South Vietnam – otherwise, I would not have been granted a visa – and joined a French group of sympathisers, mostly teachers and card-carrying members of the French Communist Party. It was a rare journalistic opportunity, the first time a small group of Western tourists had been taken on a carefully controlled tour of what was then still that most secretive of countries.

The flight, via Vientiane, took us over savage and wild countryside, steep mountains and silvery twisting rivers, landing at Hanoi's Gia Lam international airport. During the war, this had been an intensely defended air base, thick with surface-to-air missiles and anti-aircraft guns. Now a row of antiquated biplanes, helicopters and Russian turbo-props, slumbered in the tall grass; there was no sign of the Migs which had defended it. Our bus steered an erratic course through a meandering stream of cycles, jeeps and Molotova lorries, which a few months before had been running ammunition to the NVA in the south. Now the cargo was cement for reconstruction, and rice.

Hanoi was an extraordinarily industrious city. The squalid suburbs, as grim as any in Asia, smelt of desperate poverty, machines and round-the-clock production; yet, paradoxically, its densely crowded streets were strangely muted. The citizens of Hanoi – workers, soldiers, militiamen – rode only bicycles.

The bikes were a central part of Hanoi's communist uniform, like the clothes they wore, the drab olive-green shirts, the trousers, the rubber sandals and the pith helmets. No flirtatious girls in graceful *aó dài* dresses glided like dancers down these streets. It still had the drama of a wartime capital. At dawn public loudspeakers poured out martial music and exhortations to work while people did PT under the spreading tamarind trees. Compared to sultry, sophisticated,

184

brash Saigon, Hanoi – soon-to-be capital of a unified Vietnam – had a depressing dreariness. It was only many years later, on a return visit, that I realised I had been wrong and appreciated the extraordinary beauty of its crumbling colonial buildings set around the lakes and the unique quality of its people, who toiled and sweated and strived for happiness without much opportunity for expressions of individual freedom.

But for now, the strict conformity of this victorious city and the cold solemnity of Ho Chi Minh's mausoleum, with the white-gloved guards goosestepping up and down, filled me with infinite sadness. I was still raw from the falls of Saigon and Phnom Penh. It came as no surprise to learn that the Russians had helped to build the mausoleum after Ho's death in 1969 and that the first delegation to pay homage there was from the Soviet Union. The Soviet star was riding high over North Vietnam in those days and continued to do so until the Soviet Union collapsed more than a decade later.

I watched the first shift of children on their way to school at 5.30 each morning, young pioneers with red scarves knotted around the neck, as in Moscow. And a gaggle of tiny children was permanently outside the hotel, cadging tin badges of Lenin from passing Russians, who gave them with the same eagerness that the American GIs had doled out gum to shoeshine boys in Saigon in the angry and not so distant past.

During the war, almost all foreigners in Hanoi were fraternal delegates from the so-called Socialist republics and the assumption was strong, especially among the young, that any 'round-eye' was a *Lien-xo* or Russian. I found I resented this mistake. The easiest way out was to say I was French; for whom there seemed a certain

185

nostalgia among the older generation. 'You French have no money, but a heart,' they said.

We stayed at the Thong Nhat, the Unity Hotel, which during French rule had been the Métropole, much frequented by French officers. I looked for traces of the old French days – Chez Betty in the rue Paul Bert where, in 1954, *volontaires* who were not parachutists downed their last *pots* at the bar before jumping for the first time in their lives, at night, into the fiery hell of Dien Bien Phu. They were Frenchmen, *légionnaires*, but also Vietnamese, Africans all simple soldiers of the Corps Expéditionnaire – and there were always more volunteers than places in the planes. The last men into Dien Bien Phu jumped on the night of 5–6 May. Some landed in the barbed wire; one fell into the morgue near the underground hospital, where Doctor Paul Grauwin was amputating limbs without anaesthetic. Blundering through the ghostly darkness in search of his unit, he found himself hanging on to the human limbs of corpse after corpse of dead French soldiers for support. By the time he was rescued, he had drained an entire waterbottle of *pastis* and his face had a deathly tinge. A day later, on 7 May at 5.30p.m., Dien Bien Phu fell. I wondered what had become of Grauwin.

In the Hanoi museum, Major Minh, my Vietnamese guide, stolid-faced and proud, showed me a mock-up of the battle, complete with sound effects and a little red flag that popped up over the French command bunker at the end, to show it had finally been overrun. Appropriately, in this city where the bicycle was king, pride of place was given to one of the convoy of primitive machines which had ferried ammunition for the Viet Minh across hundreds of miles of jungle terrain to the front; and the copy of a message of encouragement from Winston Churchill to Général Christian de la Croix de Castries, the garrison commander, just before the end, was also on display. How pointless Churchill's message seemed now. And there at Do Son, my history lesson of what the Vietnamese communists called the Patriotic War came full circle when, unheralded, I came across a smiling General Vo Nguyen Giap, legendary victor of Dien Bien Phu and the just-ended war against the Americans, strolling along the beach, as if on holiday, a group of army officers at his side. He stopped to chat with a couple of local girls. Then he came and exchanged pleasantries with us and signed autographs on the back of Ho Chi Minh postcards before strolling on again, a slight figure but one of evident moral strength.

Even more memorable than that rare sighting of Giap was a day spent at Ha Long bay. In Saigon, my French journalist friends who had covered the Indo-China war used to talk with a far-away look in their eyes about the beauty of Ha Long. The bay had the ethereal quality of a Chinese silk screen: towering rocks covered with vegetation jutted like dragons' fangs out of fifty miles of emerald water. Coastal junks with their bat-wing sails, reddish-brown, glided through the rock-studded bay; the whole composition so peaceful and unusual that it seemed not of this world. I was not surprised that the French called it the eighth wonder of the world.

There were not many diversions during our tour, but that evening produced a gratifyingly amusing incident. A party of Czech tourists, many of them Prague intellectuals, were dining at our Do Son hotel. They befriended our French party and we were soon toasting one another and singing national songs. The Czechs became monumentally drunk and, throwing caution to the winds, burst into anti-Russian songs. Our Vietnamese hosts were bewildered and they were soon out of their depth as the jokes and songs took on a vigorously hostile, anti-Soviet tone; they looked down at the floor in evident embarrassment. Eventually, the Soviet technicians staying in the hotel stood up as one and stomped into the night; then even the card-carrying members of the French Communist Party had the courage to raise a cheer.

The road back to Hanoi carried us through rice fields refreshed with rain, past abandoned concrete pill-boxes, sad and decaying vestiges of the French war, part of a chain of defences the Foreign Legion had built in the Red River Delta. I was ruminating on the impossible courage of that French war when Major Minh, our stern-faced guide who was sitting next to me, started to talk. He lectured me about the crimes committed by the American forces in South Vietnam, in particular how there had been an American campaign to destroy the Vietnamese race by lacing 33, the local beer, with a sterilising agent. I thought things had gone far enough and told him that he could rightly accuse the US forces of all kinds of atrocities, but genocide, through a secret sterilisation programme of the local beer was not one of them and it was ridiculous to insist otherwise. The cat was well and truly out of the bag, and I owned up to my wicked past as a member of the capitalist press who for the past five years had worked as a journalist in Saigon.

I fully expected to be expelled; on the contrary, Minh and I subsequently had a series of most sensible conversations about the war, and at the end of the trip he stood up, his tight mouth breaking into a wide smile, and told the assembled members of the French Communist Party that there was among its group only one foreigner worthy of membership of the Vietnamese Communist Party. That was – pointing a pudgy finger at me – Ong [Monsieur] Jon Swain.

The Vietnamese are an exasperating people, but they can be full of the oddest surprises.

Alas, of Chez Betty and other places there was not a trace. No one remembered them; my questions were met by blank silence.

Many nights, I sat in my little house opposite Samsen railway station and pondered the tragedy inside Cambodia's sealed borders. Many times I went up to the border, as close as the Thai soldiers would allow me to go, and gazed at the little bridge across the stream which we had crossed after Phnom Penh's fall. Many times I talked to refugees who had just come out. Cambodia's self-imposed isolation made their claims impossible to verify, but their swollen feet, torn clothes and emaciated bodies gave the reports authenticity.

The great surge of emotion that had swept the world when Phnom Penh fell to the communists had by now fallen away to silence and what was happening in Cambodia, still completely closed to outsiders, was attracting little attention or indignation. Yet I knew, in my heart, that if any country deserved the world's compassion and interest, it was Cambodia: ghastly stories were coming out of killings, atrocities and starvation. The world probably will never know how many died or had their lives irreparably broken by the Khmer Rouge's rush to forge this new society. After five years of war which killed or wounded nearly a million people – a seventh of the population – I would argue that even one was one too many.

Five years of war had been followed not by a kind of peace and stability, as in Vietnam, which was sad enough anyway, but by a year of grim revolution. Kaj Bjork, Sweden's ambassador to Peking, was the only westerner allowed to visit the country and glimpse what was happening. When he returned from Cambodia, he reported that the Khmer Rouge revolution had been 'more radical and far-reaching than either the Chinese or Russian revolutions'. The countrywide upheaval had been planned long in advance by these dour radicals under their leader Pol Pot. It was a revolutionary imperative – the surest, fastest way to destroy the old 'exploitive society' of the towns. The Khmer Rouge saw no need to move at a slower, kindlier pace.

It was now clear that their revolution had obliterated what little progress had been made in the past hundred years and was in the process of destroying an ancient civilisation which had stayed intact for centuries. The US embassy in Thailand, which had set up a monitoring team on the Thai-Cambodia border, was rashly saying that the worst Khmer Rouge excesses were over. How wrong they turned out to be. The worst was yet to come.

But to get a better picture, as 17 April approached, the first anniversary of the 'liberation', I drove up to Surin province of Thailand to stay with Bizot, to try to make some sense of the Cambodian tragedy. It was a long drive and I arrived as the sun sank and darkness closed over the fields. I found the Frenchman living in a wooden house in the little town of Prasat, about thirty kilometres from the Cambodian frontier.

As I walked down the lane into his garden, a bucket of water thrown by a giggling Thai girl hit me full in the face. It was the Songkran Water Festival, celebrating the Thai New Year, and *farangs* were choice targets for the traditional soaking.

I had to smile – the Frenchman had not changed one bit. He was still perfectly in tune with his surroundings. Thanks to the Khmer Rouge, he had seen his work in Cambodia rendered futile. He had lost thousands of irreplaceable books. He had lost his Cambodian family and his house. Yet here he was in a faded sarong, his boxer

dog Avi at his side, still surrounded by girls and immersed once
more in his Khmer Buddhist texts. We sat up late into the night,
our minds flying back to the fall of Phnom Penh, our confinement
in the embassy, the sad partings. Hélène, his daughter, was safely in
France, but of her mother – banished to the countryside – there
was no news. However, Bizot was getting fleeting information from
Cambodians trickling across the border; what they told him chilled
the heart.

At the end of the war, most refugees wished only to return to
their villages, to rebuild their homes, to farm and pick up the threads
of their old lives. The Khmer Rouge had denied them this right and
dispossessed them. It had forced them out into the countryside at
gunpoint and made them settle and work in strange and sometimes
distant places. It had severed their links with the past in all sorts
of ways. In particular, it had done away with traditional musical
instruments, abolished festivals, burned books and records and confiscated Buddhist manuscripts. Bizot, familiar with Cambodian culture, said the Khmer Rouge had robbed the people of Cambodia of
life's few pleasures. Phnom Penh radio frequently reported that
Cambodia was a country of 'genuine happiness'. However, the
Khmer Rouge had sacrificed gaiety and spontaneity for uniform
drabness. What used to be an elaborate, joyful marriage ceremony
steeped in Buddhist tradition had been replaced by a cold handshake.
There were no schools for the children, and the character as well as
the mood of the country was changing.

New villages, built to accommodate the tens of thousands of
people driven into the countryside and forced to fend for themselves,
were of a tedious style. The wooden houses on stilts, with their
Buddhist corner shrines and floors polished by years of bare feet,

had been condemned as decadent and bourgeois and were fast vanishing. With them went the soul of the Cambodian village. In their place, the Khmer Rouge were said to be making the people build wooden shacks close to the ground, not where the peasant wanted – on winding paths to confuse the evil spirits – but laid out in tidy rows, like a housing estate. It was a way of deepening the gulf between the present and the past and controlling the people employed in the new collectives. Meanwhile, in empty Phnom Penh the Khmer Rouge leadership was doing very nicely, living in the trim French villas around the embassies.

Everything now pointed to Cambodia remaining closed and withdrawn into itself for a long time, until the Khmer Rouge had attained the goals of their revolution. These were to turn Cambodia into a strong, independent country which, to quote Phnom Penh radio, had 'neither rich nor poor, exploiter nor exploited', was economically self-supporting and beholden to nobody. But what was plain was that these changes had been so radical, the sacrifices demanded of the people so great, that it was hard for Cambodians to believe they were living in the country of their birth. With the passing of time their wounds might heal, but for the present they ranked among the saddest people on earth.

On Bizot's advice, I drove along the border road on the Thai side to the ruins of the great Khmer temple of Preah Vihear, on top of an escarpment closed in by forest which was Thai territory. The temple was Cambodian and was held by a detachment of Khmer Rouge soldiers; above it floated the blood-red flag of their Democratic Kampuchea. Five hundred yards away, the Thai military manned a hilltop position with machine guns. This was as close as I was allowed, and from it I could look down on Cambodia.

It was a blistering hot day and the Thai soldiers were sheltering from the heat, but I was determined to see Cambodia and stepped out of the thickly wooded jungle. Below me was the whole of the vast north Cambodian plain, open and brown in the heat, but without visible signs of life. Nothing moved; not a living thing, not even a thread of smoke from a village fire. It was deathly still. For more than an hour, I sat staring into this void, my head filled with memories. Inevitably my thoughts turned to Pran. As I gazed down on the barren and uninhabited countryside, I asked myself was he dead, or was he somewhere beyond my vision, trapped and toiling in the giant labour camp Cambodia had become?

The Eyes of Vietnam

Little by little, a curtain now began to rise on a new Indo-Chinese horror. The war in Vietnam was over. The Americans and the army of South Vietnam had been defeated. The country was unified. The killing had stopped. But in a sense there was something more murderous than gunfire. Many people, indeed many ordinary people, ignorant of politics, were in despair. They were suffering greatly, their spirits crushed by the creed of communism and a continuous rotting of the system. A dark hopelessness filled their souls. And so first hundreds, then thousands of Vietnamese put to sea in small fishing boats from the heavily guarded shores of Vietnam.

Each boatload was representative of Vietnam's unhappy post-war society: there were teachers, writers, lawyers, students, former soldiers and young men of draft age. There were aircraft mechanics and shopkeepers and single mothers who fled because of official discrimination against their Amerasian children, the offspring of American GIs. There were whores; there were farmers and fishermen and, sometimes, there were disillusioned former Viet Cong fleeing the regime they fought so fiercely to install. The communist government often encouraged them to leave, regarding them as potential troublemakers. Many of the refugees were ethnic Chinese, former businessmen from Cholon, Saigon's Chinatown, who were being persecuted by Vietnam's vociferously anti-Chinese post-war government.

After a special UN conference, Hanoi was forced to abandon its policy of evicting its unwanted Chinese and to adopt a programme of 'orderly departures' by air. But there were also numerous disenchanted Vietnamese who regarded escape, preferably to the United States, as the only hope the future held. Desperately they put to sea in unseaworthy boats.

Many did not live to taste the freedom they sought. Just hours after they sailed from little fishing ports in the Mekong Delta of southern Vietnam, they found rape, robbery and a watery death in the Gulf of Thailand.

The pirates who attacked them were Thai fishermen. Piracy has prospered in the waters of the Gulf of Thailand for centuries, but falling fish catches, rising fuel costs, and the presence of gold and of defenceless and attractive women turned these law-abiding fishermen into monsters. The suffering of the Vietnamese boat people was almost beyond imagination; it consumed anyone who came into contact with it; for years after the war was over, I found myself coming back again and again to the subject and visiting the camps, principally in Thailand, where they were held. World opinion was slow to react to the horrors of piracy, however. The camps were controlled by the Thai army and visitors needed an official pass and an escort. But sometimes it was possible to sneak in, in the guise of an aid worker; then the Vietnamese would open their hearts, secure in the knowledge that they were not being eavesdropped on by the Thais.

I was astonished to find boat people who appeared to have come to terms with the horror of their flight and could talk dispassionately about their ordeals even to a complete stranger like myself. However, one day I met a mother who had virtually lost the will to live, a tragic representative of all their suffering. A Thai policeman had pulled her by the hair from the hold of a boat where she was hiding and had deliberately thrown her baby son into the water to drown when she resisted. And I still think back with sorrow to sixteen-year-old La Kieu Ly, soft-faced and graceful; she was the sole survivor of a boat raided by pirates.

I met her in a dead-end refugee camp in Thailand near the Cambodian border. Her desperation and grief were reflected in the candle she was offering up at the camp's makeshift Catholic church. 'It is for Kim,' she said. Kim was her sister. Though barely ten years old, she was raped repeatedly by the pirates and was presumed to have drowned. Then Ly told me what had happened. One night, she said, she had slipped out of the Vietnamese fishing village of An Giang in a twenty-four foot fishing boat. Altogether, there were twenty-two people tucked out of sight below decks, including her aunt and a younger sister. A few hours out to sea, the boat ran into some Vietnamese fishermen, who confiscated their money and gold in return for allowing them to proceed. Thirty-six hours later, they met a Thai fishing boat whose crew gave them canned fish and sweets. A few hours afterwards they were attacked by another Thai fishing boat, this time with a crew of pirates aboard. It rammed their boat twice until it sank. The pirates plucked six girls, including Ly, her aunt and Kim, out of the sea. Everyone else they left to drown, including the men, whom they drove off with knives.

Then the terror began. The girls became the pirates' playthings, repeatedly raped and terrorised with fists, hammers and knives. After tiring of them, the pirates threw the three older girls overboard. They clubbed and beat Ly. And Kim, her little sister, was raped by three fishermen in succession. Ly could hear her screams. Her last memory of Kim was of a sobbing, pain-racked little bundle of humanity, begging for life. No trace of Kim was ever found.

Ly struggled so hard that the pirates threw her, too, into the sea. Naked but for a pirate's shirt and a shawl, she kept afloat for nine hours until another Thai fishing boat rescued her. The immense generosity of these men matched the immense cruelty of the pirates. They nursed her back to life, and when they landed at the southern Thai port of Nakhon Si Thammarat, they handed Ly over to the police who sent her to the Vietnamese boat people camp at Ban Thad.

I met her there one sad Sunday morning in a small comfortless room next to the church, through Joakim Dao, president of the camp's Catholic community, and heard her story. She told me that even now, and throughout her life, she would be looking out of the window for her little sister Kim, though she knew in her heart that Kim would never be coming home. As I left the church, apologising for my unwarranted intrusion, I remember thinking with humility how she reflected the special dignity of Vietnamese women and their instinct of survival.

But when I looked into her eyes they were expressionless. They were dead. They were the eyes of Vietnam – the eyes of someone who had born the unbearable.

On another occasion, travelling along the coast of southern Thailand, I came across a group of ten men, women and children, wading ashore on the beach at Ya Ring. Shocked and physically exhausted after repeated pirate attacks, they collapsed in a huddle on the sand, all that remained of a boatload of thirty-seven refugees raided by pirates. They were all wet through and looked like drowned rats. But something about one girl was different and yet disturbingly familiar. With a jolt of recognition and sadness, I realised why she had caught my attention. She had blue eyes and brown hair. She was an Amerasian. Her name was Chung Thi Ai Ngoc. She was thirteen, and she needed urgent medical treatment; the pirates had thought her western features were a prize to be fought over, and she had been repeatedly raped.

In due course I asked Ngoc about her American father, and how she felt about going to America. She looked down at her bare feet in the sand and said nothing. Then she began to cry. She had never known her father, she said; he had gone away a few months before she was born. At the end of his Vietnam tour, he had gone home leaving her pregnant mother to fend for herself and his baby. Her mother had raised her as best she could and had only one dream, getting to America. So they had escaped by boat. And her mother? Ngoc was sobbing like a baby now, her shoulders shaking uncontrollably and her hands clenched tightly. 'I don't know where she is,' she said. The pirates had put her mother on a different boat. During the night the two boats had become separated at sea; her mother was lost to her.

In the cruel roulette of life Ngoc seemed to be an especially tragic loser. More than an innocent victim, she was a metaphor for America's intervention in Vietnam, made for the best of motives but which brought about terrible death and destruction and in the end more tragedy than it can possibly have been worth. The Americans courted the south Vietnamese assiduously; they made them dependent, then abandoned them to their fate. That is precisely what happened to Ngoc's mother; her GI boyfriend made her pregnant, then one day – like America – he jilted her and went away. When I looked into Ngoc's tear-filled eyes I saw that they, too, were the eyes of Vietnam.

I had been hearing sinister stories about the goings on at Koh Kra, an island in the Gulf of Thailand much frequented by Thai fishermen-turned-pirates. On this jagged finger of jungle-capped rock forty miles from the Thai coast and directly on the route from Vietnam to Thailand, the pirates committed their worst atrocities.

When I got to Koh Kra, it was deserted, having been cleaned up by the United Nations and Thai police raids. I quickly saw though that it stood out as a monument to all the suffering of the boat people. The evidence of the pirates' occupation remained on its sandy beach; the charred carcasses of two wooden refugee boats, women's hair, a girl's shoe, bloodstained clothing and a torn bra. There were charcoal inscriptions in Vietnamese on the walls of the white hut, the only shelter on the island, and more poignant messages in paint on the rocks.

'When your boat reaches the island, immediately send all the women to hide in the bushes and caves. Don't let the Thai pirates see them. If they do they will rape them,' said one inscription. 'They will give you something to eat, but they will take everything you own, even your clothes,' said another. 'They will rape you, one boat after another, one hundred boats altogether, taking turns coming to the girls.'

In the face of such horrors, a singular man set an epic example. Theodore Schweitzer, a Missouri-born American was for a while the UN field officer at Songkhla refugee camp in the south of Thailand

– a job which need not have demanded much initiative. But he saw piracy as a curse, its eradication a challenge, and in twenty-seven daring missions to Kra he rescued nearly 1500 stranded Vietnamese refugees at great risk to himself.

In his first dramatic rescue, Schweitzer swam the best part of a mile from his boat to the island at two in the morning. In the best Hollywood tradition, he rose from the sea and confronted a group of pirates gang-raping refugee women on the beach. He had only a commando knife with which to defend himself against this ruthless bunch. But his unexpected arrival and tough air of authority unnerved the pirates and probably saved his life. That night, he rescued 157 distraught refugees. One was a badly burned woman who had been hiding from the pirates in high grass when they poured petrol on it and set it alight. Another woman was so terrified of being gang-raped again that she stood in sea water up to her knees in a rock cave and stifled her screams of pain as giant crabs bit at her legs. Claude Bordes, a French doctor who treated her, told me she would bear the scars for life.

One of the most barbaric pirate attacks on Kra happened a few days before I arrived when more than 200 fishermen–turned–pirates attacked and towed Vietnamese refugee boats to the island. The fishermen raped more than fifty women and teenage girls and killed sixteen of them. Such incidents affected the tough American deeply. In a moving interview, he described the death in hospital of a Vietnamese girl in her early teens shortly after he had rescued her from Kra. 'She died of shock and convulsion,' he said. 'Her jaw locked open. She died from fear. She was just totally scared to death. She was a very beautiful little girl and the pirates picked on her every time.'

203

Nothing better captures the sorrow in the souls of these victims than the simple message I saw scrawled in charcoal on a hut wall on Kra. It read: 'Moment of remembering father and mother,' and was signed Tran Van Sang. Another said: 'Remembering twenty-one days' suffering of three sisters.'

More than ten years later, to international indifference, Vietnamese in their thousands were still putting to sea in small boats to escape poverty and oppression at home. And so, not very long ago, I spent two unforgettable days with a group of boat people whose thirty-seven-day struggle for survival in a drifting boat was as harrowing as any I have ever encountered, and quite beyond the range of most people's experiences.

I met them at Puerto Princesa on the lovely Philippines island of Palawan, where an asylum camp for boat people waiting to be resettled in the West had been established. It was not Vietnam; it might have been. A frenzy of green trees tumbled down to a sandy beach and a turquoise sea. The air was scented with the smell of woodsmoke and cooking. There was a little Catholic church, there were dimly lit noodle shops and masses of ragged children, laughing and tumbling in the mud, for it was the rainy season. There were pretty women, generous with their smiles. There were boy scout groups, lovers sitting on a bench and ageing men with wispy beards and wrinkled faces and sad, watery eyes. It had the chaotic intimacy of a fishing port on the Mekong.

Early in the morning in a quiet corner of the camp, I sat down with Dinh Thong Hai, a thirty-year-old tailor from Saigon, and Vo

Thi Bach Yen, a seamstress from the Mekong Delta. As we drank *cà phê sữa*, filtered coffee sweetened with condensed milk, out of grimy glasses, I was struck by how sad they were. Both had left Vietnam desperately looking forward to a future in America. It was Hai's fifteenth escape attempt. He had been jailed several times for trying to flee. Yen's husband, a former captain in the defeated Saigon army, and her two older children had been in California for more than a year and she had escaped from Vietnam with her four-year-old daughter to join them. Now, in front of me, they blurted out the story of their barbaric voyage in a drifting boat.

Their forty-five foot long riverboat had left Ben Tre, in the Mekong Delta, in chaos, overloaded with 110 men, women and children crammed on board with only enough food and water for a few days. It was bound for Malaysia, six days away across the ocean. But after barely two days a storm had blown up, the boat sprang a leak, the motor failed. The passengers rigged a makeshift sail and prayed for deliverance. Day after day, they were passed by merchant ships, some within hailing distance. They scrawled an SOS with toothpaste on a piece of wood and held it up; at night they made bonfires of their clothes. One night, a Japanese freighter came within a hundred yards. Several refugees, maddened by hunger and thirst, jumped into the water and swam towards it but the ship sailed on, leaving them to drown.

Panic set in as they ran out of food. Phung Quang Minh, a former corporal in the Saigon air force, forcibly established his leadership in the drifting boat. He surrounded himself with a group of followers, mostly teenagers, and they armed themselves with sticks and knives and carried out his orders in return for extra food and water seized from the weaker passengers. Even the captain of the fishing boat deferred to Minh's authority. One dawn, he jumped over the side with his daughter and three relatives and vanished in the ocean swell.

On the fourteenth day a twenty-two-year-old man died of thirst and his body was committed to the deep. On the fifteenth day, Yen's daughter died. She was one of seven small children to perish that day and was the focus of Yen's life. 'She did not say anything. She just stopped breathing,' Yen said quietly. 'The next day I asked two passengers in the boat to help me to put her little body into the sea.'

During the next days, several people began drinking sea water and their own urine, which hastened their deaths. Others toppled into the sea, jumped overboard and swam away, or clung to pieces of wood or oil drums, convinced by the seagulls circling overhead that land was nearby.

A few days later, their spirits rose when they were spotted by the USS *Dubuque*. As the 8800-ton American amphibious landing ship circled, four refugees jumped into the sea and swam towards it. One drowned; the others reached the ship only to be rebuffed by the sailors, who leaned over the side to tell them it was on a secret mission (to the Arabian Gulf) and they could not come aboard. They threw down three life-jackets and told the refugees to swim back to the boat.

In full view of the American ship, the body of a refugee who had died was thrown overboard. Sailors photographed the corpse floating in the water. One Vietnamese-speaking American told them, 'We will never let anyone on your boat die again.' The Americans gave them six cases of tinned meat, boxes of apples, plastic containers of fresh water and a map with directions to the Philippines, 250 miles away. Although the Vietnamese explained to the sailor that the boat had broken down no one offered to repair the engine. Two hours later the *Dubuque* sailed away, leaving them to their fate.

The suffering now became unendurable. Minh confiscated the American food. He beat Yen about the head with a shoe to stop her giving water to dying children. Then, twelve days after the encounter with the *Dubuque*, he and his gang turned on the others and began to murder them, one by one.

The first victim to be killed and eaten was Dao Cuong, the best friend of Hai and one of the feeblest on the boat. The refugees were dying at the rate of one or two a day; but Minh's gang preferred to kill rather than feast on the corpses of those who had died. Two children, aged eleven and fourteen, and a twenty-two-year-old woman, were his other victims. One of the children was Hai's cousin.

For the first time in almost an hour Hai and Yen were both silent for a moment. I thought they did not want to talk about it any more, because the memories of the cannibalism were too painful to recall, especially to a stranger. But then Yen took a deep breath, sighed and went on: 'It was horrible, but we did not have the strength to stop him.'

Another difficult pause, then Hai was saying: 'Two days before it happened, Cuong was so driven by hunger that he gave Minh a gold ring in exchange for an apple. But Minh's group came with knives and sticks and said they needed my friend for food to help the others to survive. I said, "No, Cuong is still alive. I cannot let you kill and eat him. You can use him if he dies." Cuong overheard the conversation. He said he did not agree to be killed. He still believed we would be rescued the next day. But the men had made up their minds. We were too weak to resist. "Kill him, kill him," one said.

"Quickly, quickly, it's almost night." And when I saw the two men grab Cuong by the feet and realised they were about to kill him, I asked them to allow us a few minutes in private. Cuong had told me before we had left Vietnam he wanted to be a Catholic. I scooped up some sea water, poured it over his head and read the Bible. Then the men pushed Cuong's head under the water until he drowned, before eating his body.'

A silence intervened. Hai's face was suddenly very pale. But the whole story was not yet out, for he said that an eleven-year-old boy – his cousin – was Minh's last victim, killed the day before their rescue by Filipino fishermen. The boy still had the strength to move and understood what was happening. 'I don't want to die. I don't want to die,' he screamed and hid in the cabin. Minh dragged him out and handed him over to his men. They held him over the side of the boat while he struggled and screamed and kicked; it took them about three minutes to drown him. Then they took out a knife, cut off the head, dismembered the body, cooked the flesh and distributed it.

Hai stopped talking. The whole story was out. A terrible sadness filled the air. I saw the shame in their faces and felt guilty that I had made them relive their experience. The significance of what Hai had been saying suddenly dawned on me. Probably they had all become cannibals to survive that terrible voyage; perhaps some of the people on that boat had, in desperation, eaten the flesh of Minh's victims and not just some part of the naturally dead. There have been reports before of cannibalism at sea; starving boat people who ate the dead. But never before, as far as I know, had there been a case of boat people murdering and eating each other to survive.

I sought to talk to Minh but UN refugee officials responsible for the camp would not allow it. He and six members of his gang were shut in a locked building guarded by Filipino soldiers and out of bounds to the rest of the camp's 4800 inmates, while their future was decided. Some of the best legal brains of the Philippines were arguing whether they should be prosecuted. Clearly it was not a normal case of murder. The desperate circumstances raised complex questions. The refugee status of the Vietnamese and the fact that the deaths had occurred at sea compounded the issue. Minh's defence was the plea of necessity. He argued that twelve days after the *Dubuque* had steamed off and left them helplessly adrift in a leaking and disabled boat, the refugees had lost all semblance of sanity and were driven by desperation to killing and cannibalism.

As I got up to go, I looked into Hai's eyes. They were black pools of horror. The eyes of the dead. This man too had eyes I cannot forget. The eyes of Vietnam.

Of the 110 refugees who left Vietnam fifty-eight died en route, *most by drowning and starvation. After investigating whether the* Dubuque *should have given more help to the refugees, the US navy suspended Captain Alexander Balian from his command and later court-martialled him. Hai and Yen have left the Philippines and are learning to live with their memories in their new lives.*

Kidnapped

I tried to give this day to you . . .
or at least a part of it.
From the top bunk I have memorised
everything you've written me . . .
this must be the hardest time
because I'm not even sure
I ever knew you . . .
through the time zones
the different days
are not really ours to give . . .
so we end up keeping them
for ourselves
and we look for other gifts.

More and more, I was waking up to the fact that without Indo-China, Southeast Asia no longer held the same attractions for me; by staying alone in Bangkok, with Jacqueline in Paris, I had cut my life in two. But a decision was made for me. In May 1976, the *Sunday Times* offered a temporary solution to my dilemma with a three month assignment in London. Six years after I had first left Paris for Cambodia, I came back to Europe, a stranger.

I flew first to Paris. After a longish spell in the wilds of the East, there could be no more wonderful city to coax the exile back to Europe. The reunion with Jacqueline was magical. She threw her arms round me. The intervening sorrows dropped away and it was as it had always been. Spring had come to Paris; the city was bursting with light and love. Like young lovers, we wandered over the uneven cobbles, pausing every now and then for long, long kisses. There was so much to catch up on, not very much time in which to do it. One evening, we went back to the Rosebud, my favourite bar, for a sentimental drink. I had hardly sat at the bar when Gilles, the white-coated barman, leant across and gripped my hand like an old friend. 'Comment va! Monsieur Jon? Ça fait bien longtemps, n'est ce pas?' I felt humbled that Gilles had recognised me at all, after all my years abroad. It was gratifying to find that in that way the Parisian atmosphere had hardly changed in my absence.

After Paris, I did not feel the same joy of homecoming in London. In five years I had spent only a few weeks in England and felt utterly removed from it. I had been named 1975 Journalist of the Year for my coverage of Cambodia, the youngest person to receive the award. Edward Heath, the ex-prime minister made the presentation. Also recognised that year were two good friends, Martin Woollacott of the *Guardian* for international reporting, and John Edwards of the *Daily Mail*, who said of his life as a reporter 'I've stood on so many doorsteps, I think of myself as a milk-bottle'. By contrast, I gave an incoherent little speech; the award evoked too many sad memories of a now distant war. It was nonetheless the highest accolade of the trade of journalism.

In the days that followed, I was homesick for the warm humanity of the streets of Asia; *ennui* weighed heavily on me and, as I joined the pressured throngs on the London Underground each day, I feared I would not get away again before I became tied down, crushed by what I dreaded most: a routine English existence. I did not want a settled life; in Indo-China I had grown accustomed to living on the edge of insecurity and it made me wary of the feel of permanence in London.

Before leaving Paris for London, I had explained to Jacqueline that we would soon be able to make up for all the lost time apart. What hollowness lay in those words, though I spoke them sincerely and directly. Out of the blue, in London, I was asked by the paper to carry out a reporting assignment behind the lines in Ethiopia. Since

April, the Derg – Ethiopia's military government – had been mobilis-
ing thousands of peasants, arming them with staves, axes and old-
fashioned guns, and trucking them up to the border of the northern
province of Eritrea to put down a rebellion there. My assignment
was to cover the war from the rebel side.

I fell into the fatal trap of many foreign correspondents – not
knowing how to turn down an assignment. The desire to cover stories
is sometimes irresistibly powerful; this ruthlessness for 'getting the
story' over and above all else, including love, has wrecked the personal lives of many colleagues; in my case, too, it was to have deep
and lasting consequences.

After all the time apart, I had a genuine desire to be with Jacqueline; yet I obstinately felt as well that I wanted to satisfy my need
to go to Ethiopia. It was a confusing time. Looking back, I suppose
I wanted a change, but had not yet fathomed what that change
should be. There was still a restlessness in my spirit, added to which
I did not know how to say no to a challenge and the paper was
insistent. Perhaps I was also feeling too insecure about my position
on a famous newspaper to turn down such an important assignment,
complex and dangerous though it was. I was carrying the burden of
a much-coveted honour and feeling my way in a city I hardly knew,
among unfamiliar colleagues with whom I had little in common.
The impulse to go was strong. There was an irreconcilable conflict
of interest in my life, another of those idiocies that had come to
litter it.

In short, the same old demons plagued me. So I explained gently
to Jacqueline that the assignment was a short one, for two or three
weeks only, and afterwards we would be able to be together. I wanted
to make things easy for her. I had hopes of us living together in

Paris in the future. I tried to explain that the separations were peripheral to the core of our existence. What we had lived through together in Indo-China was the essential. It belonged uniquely to us and was strong enough to resist all barriers of time and place. She had been suffocated with grief when she left Indo-China. My return had begun to restore her *joie de vivre* and her face had an eager and expectant look once again. But now her expression saddened and she turned very quiet. I knew that I had hurt her. In the end she stifled her bitter disappointment, as she always had, and said she understood, though how could she? She promised to be supremely patient.

My talk of togetherness turned out to be another false dream. Hardly had I arrived in Ethiopia, when I was kidnapped by guerrillas. I was held captive in the desert for the next three months on suspicion of being an 'imperialist spy'. In terms of human experience, I had faced a lot, but Ethiopia was the most dismal time in my life, worse than facing death on the muddy banks of the Mekong a year before. Even today I feel faintly sick as I relive the misery of my capture.

In the years following my captivity, the kidnapping of journalists became a vogue, especially in the Middle East. I was never in the dire situation of those who were held hostage and disappeared in the 'Black Hole' of Beirut in the 1980s to be released years later. But I have always felt a bond with them and a mutual understanding at having – briefly – faced a common, though lesser, fate. I look back on the whole distasteful interlude with weary bleakness and shudder at my decision to go.

However, Ethiopia was one of the few countries outside Asia

which fascinated me; otherwise I would have been much more wary of going. It was the country of Rider Haggard, and of Evelyn Waugh's *Scoop*. I had first come across it in a bizarre and romantic way while working for AFP in Paris some years before. Bill Smith, a distinguished Ghanaian who had once worked with Kwame Nkrumah before he was deposed and who was now on AFP's Africa desk, entranced me with descriptions of the beauty of the Ethiopian women he had met in Addis Ababa while covering Organisation of African Unity (OAU) summits. One day, in Paris, one of those Ethiopians walked into the office. Bill introduced me to her. She was Tabotu Wolde Michael, a beautiful minor member of the deposed Ethiopian royal family. When I met her she was in Paris at a silky tongued French official's invitation.

While accompanying President Georges Pompidou on his recent visit to Ethiopia, the official had spotted Tabotu at Addis Ababa's television studios. She was more than just another beautiful *nana* to be bedded. She was intelligent, the first woman in Africa to be a television news presenter, yet she had never set foot outside the African continent. The Frenchman persuaded her to join a journalist-training scheme in Paris sponsored by the French government. His intentions were more lecherous than journalistic, as Tabotu found out soon enough; on her first day in Paris, he tried to put his hand up her skirt and from then on she kept her distance.

Tabotu was tall, olive-skinned, with tousled black hair – a wild but sophisticated beauty. We became friends. I remember taking her to dinner at La Coupole, where she walked through the crowded restaurant with the splendour of a princess. Her poise turned every male head and as she passed the diners fell silent.

I saw her again in Addis. She was now married and had just had

217

her first baby. Otherwise, she was the same self-assured talkative Tabotu. Taking a risk, too, in those suspicion-ridden anti-Western days, for she invited me to dinner at home with her husband. I spent a few days in Addis, discreetly gathering as much information about the military situation as I could from diplomats and fellow-journalists. Then, sufficiently briefed, I headed north at the start of my assignment. As a precaution, I hid my Eritrean guerrilla accreditation under the carpet of my room – number 123 – at the Ras Hotel, together with a list of possibly compromising contacts. I fully expected to be back after four days. For all I know, nearly twenty years later the papers are still there.

On the third day, I was travelling in a decrepit Bedford bus through the northern part of Tigre province, which, according to legend, was once the heart of the Queen of Sheba's kingdom. All the way from Axum, the bus had been swaying perilously through a desolate landscape of bare, eroded mountains and huge granite rocks. It was top-heavy, overfilled with peasants and an indescribable collection of belongings stuffed into every nook and cranny. It seemed at times as if it would plunge over the side, as the driver, desperately manipulating wheel and gears, threw it round hairpin bends. The collective faith of the passengers must have kept it on the winding mountain road and by mid-morning, the roughest part of the journey was over. With Mkele, my destination, a couple of hours away, I nodded off to sleep.

My neighbour woke me. The bus had halted at a bend in the road. A group of armed men were running towards it across the open ground. I could not tell whether they were *shiftas* (Ethiopian bandits) or guerrillas fighting the military government. Whoever they were, they spelt trouble. I felt a spasm of fear, a feeling that I was once

218

again standing on the edge, looking down into the yawning abyss of death.

They barked orders. The passengers got out of the bus. As we stepped down into the harsh sunlight, an Ethiopian who had been sitting next to me whispered: 'Don't worry. These are good people and will not harm you.' I did not reply. As the only European, I was an inevitable target. At best, I would be taken prisoner. At worst, I would be shot. In the seconds that followed, I racked my brain for a solution. There was no way out. The passengers gathered sheepishly in a clearing by the side of the road. I mingled with them, summoning my courage to appear unconcerned. The gang leader looked us over. His eyes settled on me. He looked boyish, not much more than twenty. His AK47 rifle was pointing threateningly at my chest and in English called me over. Slowly, I moved towards him. As I stepped away from the safety of the crowd, and walked across the stony ground, the guns of his men, dark-faced, hostile and silent, followed me.

No one in the circle of passengers behind me moved or spoke. Their stillness was no security either. An almost unendurable mood of tension hung over them. Everyone was a silent onlooker to the possible killing of a foreigner. Standing in front of the guerrilla chief, I made a big effort and held out my hand. I looked into his eyes and introduced myself. There was a moment of hesitation; then he took my hand suspiciously in his. 'We are fighters of the Tigre People's Liberation Front,' he said in excellent English. 'We are going to hold you for questioning for two or three days.'

It was useless to protest or offer resistance. My friendly and unruffled manner in those first critical moments had done much to break the ice. I had disarmed the guerrillas, but my apprehension remained. As the wasted days stretched into wasted weeks of captivity, it never left me.

The guerrillas marched me away across rough country. We moved through the hot hills in a long line, the leader, Shawit, setting a cracking pace in his khaki shorts and sandals. I stumbled along in the middle, prodded with a rifle, a guerrilla at the back carrying my luggage.

That evening, the first of three months of captivity, we halted at a village. The peasants stared from the open doors of their rough stone huts. The children huddled together, afraid to approach the first European they had seen. There was no comfort in their dark faces, but no hostility either; only a shy curiosity.

Now the questioning began. The guerillas searched my body and my luggage, confiscating my passport and personal documents attesting to my being a staff correspondent of the *Sunday Times*. 'How do we know these aren't forged?' one man, bearded like Che Guevara, asked. 'We're not racists. But we have to be careful of foreigners like you in this area. We know some of them are spies of imperialism employed by the CIA and British Intelligence to inform on us. If you're innocent, you have nothing to fear.'

I protested vigorously – but politely – at being kidnapped, explaining why I was in this northern part of Tigre province not far from the border with Eritrea. I had been sent out specially from England by the *Sunday Times* to report on the progress of the peasant army sent to attack Eritrea, units of which were reportedly camped near the border. I explained that, hoping to see them, I had joined the local bus from Axum to Mkele. I sensed that they did not really believe my story. 'If you really are a journalist,' they finally said, 'we'll hear it on the BBC.'

220

*

In the event, it turned out that my assignment was already dead news. The great peasant march I had been sent to write about was over, destroyed two weeks earlier at Zalembesa, a boulder-strewn plain a day's march from where I was. It had been a colossal slaughter, I gathered. The Ethiopian army had brought up the peasants in commandeered trucks and buses. It had issued them with flintlocks, ammunition, spears, staves and some food and told them that, once inside Eritrea, they could plunder, rape and steal. At dawn the guerrillas on the heights fired down onto the crowded camp with mortars, rockets and automatic rifles. The mass of barefooted tribesmen rose in an angry swarm and, taking up their weapons, swept forward. The Eritrean guns cut them down like swathes of corn under a sickle.

In a callous attempt to drive the rabble forward, the army behind opened fire on the fleeing remnants. By four in the afternoon, the plain was still. Guerrillas picked their way among the bodies of the dead and wounded, collecting weapons. 'You could not see the ground. You could only see dead bodies,' one said. For days afterwards, vultures pecked at the human flesh and hyenas gnawed on the bones. More than 1000 tribesmen were killed and hundreds were taken prisoner. The guerrillas' superiority in weapons had turned a battle into a massacre.

We moved again at night. Under guard, I was marched through a region of huge boulders and giddying cliffs. At three in the morning I was bundled into a peasant hut and given a mattress. The guerrillas stretched out on the ground around me, rifles at their sides.

221

Lying on the dirty mattress, I grasped the reality of my captivity. I tried to imagine what was going on in the *Sunday Times* office in London. By now, surely, they would realise I was missing and raise the alarm. In due course, the bus passengers would be bound to report that a white man had been taken into the bush at gunpoint. With luck, the connection would be made. Before leaving Addis Ababa, I had told the British embassy I was travelling north and would be back four days later. So I was confident that, one way or another, word would get back that I had been kidnapped. I reasoned that my disappearance would be reported on the BBC World Service, which would convince the guerrillas of my bona fides and lead to my release. Until that moment, it was vital I develop a bond of trust with my captors so that they would find it morally repugnant to kill me. I was wretchedly aware that these guerrilla boys wielded the power of life and death over me, so I was determined not to become an encumbrance. I knew I was expendable, as are all prisoners of hard-pressed guerrilla forces in a war.

To keep up my spirits, I thought of the fall of Phnom Penh and of how Pran had so brilliantly saved us by talking the Khmer Rouge into releasing us. There, on the banks of the Mekong, he had established a human link with the murderous guerrillas and I resolved to do the same.

Before I closed my eyes that night, I thought with emotion and remorse of Jacqueline, waiting for me in a studio in the rue Serpente on the Left Bank. I was supposed to be a stable factor in her life and I had vanished without trace. I spent the most comfortless night of my existence.

*

I awoke at dawn to an unfamiliar world of braying donkeys, yapping dogs, a peasant family watching me with fierce excitement. Hordes of near-naked children stared open-mouthed as I emerged, and then scampered into their huts. The sharp eyes of the guerrillas were on me too, so I put on a big show of enthusiasm for this second day of my captivity that, inwardly, I did not feel. This place, a collection of stone hovels, deep inside a guerrilla-held zone, was to be my home for the first three days. A woman gave me a cup of hot sweet tea. I sat on the ground and drank it. Then the questioning began again. 'Who are you? Why did you come to Tigre? Which political party do you belong to in England? What do you think of the Derg? Why does the British government support it?'

My answers were noted on a piece of paper. There was no respite. In the intervals between the questions I played with the children. It was important, too, I felt, to build up confidence between myself and this family in whose home I was a prisoner. They would surely stop anything bad happening to me.

Perhaps my best friend at this time was a precocious little girl of nine. Her mother liked me too and worried about my well-being. Instead of *injera*, the local food, a pancake which you tore off in chunks in your hand and dipped into a community saucepan of spicy gravy which I found difficult to stomach, she found me some macaroni, a legacy of Italian colonialism. 'Stay a while,' she said, 'and you can marry my daughter.' Indignant, the child did not give it a second thought: 'I don't want to marry him. I want to marry a man who's black like me,' the child replied.

Only now did I appreciate how harsh the life of these peasants was. The nearest clinic and educational services were at least two days' walk away; the nearest well three miles. I watched the women

223

come back from it every day, bent double under the burden of their pitchers, and marvelled at their stamina.

Each family farmed a tiny plot of land. The soil was stony, the water scarce, and the farmers had to give half their grain to the church and the state. The only freedom these villagers had in their lives was to breed. Even then, one out of every three of their children died in infancy from disease or malnutrition. Little wonder that the guerrillas exercised such a strong influence over peasants who worked so exhaustingly hard. More than that, I did not comprehend how people could survive amid such want.

As the days passed, I sensed the mood ease. But I was still faced with the same unknowns, chief among which was how long my captivity would last. There were one˗or two moments when I was seized by blind terror, convinced by some action, gesture or expression that the guerrillas found me a nuisance and were plotting my death. One day, I found one of my guards reading a letter to Jacqueline. He could not make sense of my tortured squiggles, but it enraged me; in an unusual flash of bravado, I tried to bash his face in. The metallic clunk of a rifle bolt driven home brought me up sharply. I looked round to see an old Lee Enfield trained on my back. Afterwards, I was watched more closely.

We marched at night for safety. From a village above Zerona, I watched government jets wheel in the sky, hit the town and rake a goatherd on a hill with cannon fire. It was a useless form of warfare which I had seen all too often in Vietnam. The belief behind it was that if you hit the peasants hard enough, they would tire of giving the guerrillas shelter, but the Vietnam experience showed that bombing only alienates the people. I doubted that the Ethiopians would find the result any different.

The frequent air attacks did have one important effect. They forced the peasants to change the pattern of their lives. Now they slept during the day and worked in the fields at night, when they were assured of empty skies.

As we marched deeper into Eritrea, I began to study my captors. Some were young members of Ethiopia's educated élite. I asked them what made them give up bright futures for the rigours of guerrilla life. 'To struggle for our people,' was the characteristic reply. I had to stifle the impulse to shout against the wooden communist rhetoric that popped up in nearly every conversation. To have done so would have been disastrous. As the days dragged on, the predictability of these heavy-handed phrases became more and more exasperating.

The guerrillas – whether Eritrean or Tigrean – led monotonous lives with few pleasures other than smoking and drinking *tatja*, the traditional drink. Plenty of girls were around, some of considerable beauty, but I saw no evidence of love affairs and divined the reason. New recruits were forced to take an oath of celibacy on joining the movement; the penalty for breaking it was death.

My future stretched like an endless road, leading nowhere. The days spread into weeks, during which I lost my purpose. We followed the same pattern – waking, marching, resting, waking, marching, resting – and seemed to make little progress. Each day we listened to the BBC World Service news. To my dismay, there was still no mention of my disappearance. I began to wonder whether I would ever be found, whether my family would ever know what had happened to me, and wept with frustration and despair.

The daily march began at about two in the morning, the five guards who accompanied me and the donkey bearing my canvas suitcase threading confidently through the mountain trails by moonlight. After dawn, the temperature would start to climb rapidly; by 9a.m., it was too hot to make decent progress. Since there was also the danger of air strikes, the guards would call a halt and we spent the heat of the day dozing in readily offered peasant huts. On these stopovers, I was too exhausted to think.

By and by, our little party reached an Eritrean People's Liberation Front (EPLF) field headquarters fifteen miles east of Asmara, the capital of Eritrea. It was set in a broad plain ringed by dark hills. I was fed and left under a bush while my guards discussed me with their Eritrean confrères. I knew it was a decisive moment and hoped it would lead to my release.

After twenty-four hours, the guerrillas reached their decision. I was to be marched southwards, back to Tigre, for another spell of captivity; not northwards, as I had hoped, towards the Sudanese border and freedom. The EPLF leadership in the camp had decided to wash their hands of my case, which I had been given no chance to argue. With simple finality, I was told I would shortly start the sixty-mile trek back, with my five guards.

I remained quiet and sullen during the return march, thinking it pointless to conceal my anger. Three days later, I was back at Zerona in a very black mood indeed. I had to convince the guerrillas to set me free. My chance came when I was summoned to see Berhu Aregawi, a founding member of the TPLF and one of the most important brains of the movement. I put the case for my release in the strongest terms I dared.

The basis of my argument was that holding a British journalist could only bring adverse publicity for the TPLF. The trouble was, he still did not know I was really a newspaperman. However, my arguments seemed to carry some weight. After keeping me in suspense while he discussed the matter with his colleagues, Berhu announced that I would be taken back to Eritrea – and that this time he would accompany me personally.

So we set off yet again, walking through the hills and dusty plains. Berhu was a strange, taciturn man. He had become a fanatical Marxist at Addis Ababa university. Tall, thin and with a wispy beard, his opinion of Britain seemed to have been fashioned by the sight of the Queen opening Axum cathedral in 1965 at a glittering ceremony during Haile Selassie's reign. He had been a boy scout at the time. In our discussions, he fiercely defended kidnapping as a legitimate political weapon. He made it clear that the sacrifice of an innocent life was less important than his political ideals.

I was careful to guard my tongue, but we still had rows. 'This is not a hotel! This is a guerrilla encampment!' he shouted at me one day when, exhausted after a thirty-two-mile march, I pleaded for a rest. He was frequently bad-tempered. But we came to respect each other and built a measure of mutual trust.

Berhu carried more clout than my previous guards. At our first stopping point – the EPLF camp where I had been turned back earlier – just a few hours of negotiation resulted in our being sent on our way northwards.

One night we skirted besieged Asmara, the echo of spasmodic gunfire in our ears, the moon sliding in and out of the clouds like a beast stalking its prey. Apparently the guerrillas could infiltrate any part of the city and had assassinated a number of Ethiopian army leaders. I associated Asmara's siege with the last days of Phnom Penh, but this time I found myself observing a guerrilla war from the other side.

We continued northwards, sometimes just the two of us, sometimes escorted; an odd nocturnal procession under a shifting moon. We marched through the mountain pass at Woki, and finally, on 13 July, after sixteen days on foot or perched on indefatigable donkeys, we reached our destination – the EPLF's main base camp in northern Eritrea. I hated every step of that march but persisted in the belief that each pace forward was a pace towards freedom; also, I was determined to give the guerrillas a taste of my walking prowess; they did not believe westerners could walk. At halts, I listened to the radio. I heard that a drought was devastating England, the greatest of the century, and laughed bitterly as I looked at the desert furnace around me. Then there was Beethoven, and Lord Peter Wimsey who kept me faintly amused. One night, we camped at a large abandoned Italian home, a simple stone structure, like a southern Italian farmhouse. The owner had left an unforgettable imprint of Italian civilisation – a beautiful orange grove set in a hollow, watered by a gurgling stream. To me it was the Garden of Eden. It was green and cheerful and the guerrillas let me drink the cool water and eat the oranges ripening on the branches. My spirits lifted. A few nights later, dog was on the menu, then donkey. For the guerrillas, the poorest meat was a luxury.

The EPLF camp lay in a long narrow valley on the edge of the desert. It consisted not of huts but of guerrilla groups, living, working and sleeping on the valley floor, under bushes, or acacia trees or inside lines of caves that riddled the slopes.

Weeks of despair and loneliness followed. My habitat was a salvadora bush on the valley floor in a landscape so hot and barren that I felt I was at the burning centre of the planet. I exchanged not more than three sentences with my captors in a day. The flies were my early alarm call around dawn. Zeray, the guard, brought tea. As the heat rose I would retreat deeper into the bush, out of the shimmering inferno. Inside the bush it was tolerable. Here, there were snakes, a family of scorpions, a chameleon. I avoided the snakes and scorpions, though more than once in the blackness I felt something caress my skin, lightly, like a leaf, and it scared me. I tried to befriend the chameleon and enjoyed forcing it to change colour. Here the stillness was immense. I had time to rethink my life. On balance, I thought, having made it so far, I would eventually be released. I was no longer so afraid of dying, alone and invisible in this desolate corner of Africa. But I thought how slender one's hold on life is in such circumstances, and how those circumstances can change. I thought of Commandant Galopin, a French officer who had parachuted into the Tibesti region of Africa, not very far from me, to negotiate the release of Madame Claustre, a French hostage. After nearly a year, her captors changed their minds about Galopin, and hanged him from the nearest tree. If the Tigreans had been the Khmer Rouge, I, too, would have been long dead.

At such times of isolation, one relies on one's inner resources for consolation. For hours each day, I rummaged in my past. I would choose a different theme, take it out of the pigeon-hole of my life, dust it, examine it and put it back. To test my earliest recollections,

I began with my childhood in the countryside of India, which is the origin of my zest for travel and quest for adventure.

Vivid pictures of India painted my eyes. Now I saw a small child lying terrified in the darkness while a great pandemonium went on in the garden outside, a deafening banging of kettles, shrieks, shouts and running. Then the soothing voice and kiss of my mother explaining, as she stroked my hair, that a leopard was prowling in our garden and that there was no need to be frightened; my father was up on the flat roof-top, trying to shoot it, and in any case I was safe between the sheets, under the mosquito net and fan. Now I saw myself coming down to breakfast the next morning and finding a leopard stretched motionless on the verandah, weeping blood over its beautiful fur. Now I saw a small boy on the back of an elephant; now the small boy playing hide and seek with the servants in the garden. One in particular, Roti, had loved to amuse me with funny games. I was his *baba sahib*.

We lived seventy miles from Calcutta, in a big whitewashed bungalow, Amlagora, famous for the sacred fossilised tree in the garden. I remember the monkeys screaming insolently from the great rain trees. Our nearest 'white' neighbour was thirty miles away and often in the hot season we would pile into the car, an old Studebaker, and drive there and back for a swim in the pool. After my *ayah* had put me to bed, my mother would come and read me a story. It was inevitably one by Kipling. Down below, there always seemed to be a party. So that I was not left out, my father would come upstairs afterwards and kiss me goodnight. Before he left, he would affectionately rub his cheek against my face. It was rough like sandpaper but I learnt to like the masculine smell of whisky and cigars his presence brought and to this day I associate it with my childhood and the strong, fearless man my father was. I remember walking beside him once and holding his leg in fright as he drew his swordstick and slashed in two a venomous snake gliding out of the bushes in our path.

Another vivid picture was the seaside holidays at Digga in the Bay of Bengal. Now I saw a small boy being driven in a Land Rover through the night, to arrive by the sea at dawn. Then the Land Rover racing to our bungalow across a flat beach turned into a rich carpet of red by millions of landcrabs scurrying to their holes. I remembered swimming with my father, the sea snakes writhing in the fishing nets, the soothing anthem of the crickets, the bears lumbering past the bungalow in the dark. Then, one day, all too soon, my Indian life came to an end. I saw a small boy arriving at his first boarding-school in the west of England just before his sixth birthday, his mother saying goodbye before returning to India for another lonely year without her children. I hid sobbing under the bed in the dormitory. It was an agonising separation for me, and as I realised later, for my mother too.

My father was manager of a vast estate in West Bengal for a large Anglo-Indian company. It was a life of great isolation but not a dull one. He stayed on and finally came back to England for good in 1957. I had not seen him for three years and he was a stranger to me. He never really settled down, and nor did I. In some mysterious way, even in those early days, I already felt an outsider in England, influenced by memories of my first years in India, a country none of my schoolfriends had ever seen and which I imbued with the wonder of adventure and romance. I wanted to get away.

My parents settled in the West Country on the edge of Dartmoor. They were keen for me to go into the services, and I did briefly consider the Royal Navy. Primarily to please them, I applied for a naval scholarship which I mercifully failed. I must have been but fifteen when I decided I would be a journalist, and a foreign correspondent at that. From that time nothing dissuaded me, not even the French Foreign Legion in which I enlisted.

What prompted an apparently normal English boy of seventeen to throw himself into the Legion was quite simply a wish to prove his worth to himself. A love affair with a French girl had gone wrong and a change of life through foreign adventure was the best cure for a broken heart. One chill, grey November morning, I presented myself at the gates of Fort de Nogent on the eastern edge of Paris where, with a sinking feeling in the stomach, I was interviewed by an abrupt adjutant.

I lied about my age, handed over my passport and, casting an apprehensive eye over a recruiting poster of a splendid *légionnaire* in white képi and scarlet epaulettes that said 'Engagez-vous dans la Légion Étrangère. Métier d'homme', I signed for five years.

The adjutant changed my name to Jack Summers, born in Epsom. This was to honour the Legion's contract of anonymity in return for signing on, for a willingness to soldier, and if called on to die for France. At the end I would receive French nationality.

In place of my civilian clothes which were taken away, I was kitted out in a beret and ill-fitting green fatigues and boots, and henceforth addressed always as Summers, so that soon I was so indoctrinated I no longer thought of myself as Jon Swain, but responded instantly and only to my pseudonym.

There were other recruits beside myself from all nationalities – Germans, Spanish, Belgian, the odd refugee from Eastern Europe, and a drunken Swedish merchant seaman who had travelled by bus from Copenhagen to Paris to enlist in the Legion for a bet.

I was the only Englishman and, as such, a source of mild curiosity. In the following days, many of the recruits were found to be unsuitable and discharged, among them the Swede with whom I had become friends; we were the only two English speakers.

I spent nearly a month at Fort de Nogent, undergoing fitness and medical examinations. We were never allowed beyond the barrack walls. We were given close military haircuts and as soon as the recruits were in sufficient numbers to undergo basic training we were transported in covered army lorries at night through the streets of Paris to the Gare de Lyon. There we were marched onto a train, crammed into special compartments under guard, and emerged early the next morning at the Gare St Charles in Marseilles. The sun was shining, but our reception was chilly – a squad of military policemen and alsatian guard dogs were lined up on the platform waiting for us.

The following weeks at Bas Fort St Nicolas, a forbidding *caserne* dominating the Vieux Port, followed an inexorable pattern: drill, X-rays, injections against typhoid, cholera, visits to the dentist, marches, the start of basic training, French lessons. Throughout there was no contact with the outside world. Our universe was the barracks, but sometimes we peeked over the battlements at the girls below, hand in hand with their men. More of us were discharged to a round of half-envious mocking from the rest of us.

The spirit of the Legion was not yet there inside us, but as we recruits became integrated into this illustrious corps through its training and discipline our national identities were subsumed. A *kamerad-schaft* developed and we looked at ourselves with a glow of pride, determined to be among the bravest of the brave. Not without reason is 'Legio Patria Nostra' the Legion's motto; our final loyalty was to it.

Over drinks in the *popotte* I listened, in awe, to the old campaigners who had fought in Indo-China. Tough and seasoned, their skin was burned the colour of leather and their eyes had a far-away look. They talked with nostalgia of the beauty of the *petites Tonkinoises* and of the Legion's epic role. They were heroic figures whom I longed to emulate and I knew then, in my inmost soul, that Indo-China would lure me.

But my destiny lay elsewhere. In the midst of basic training I was summoned one day to an interview by a commandant with the Deuxième Bureau, the French army's intelligence unit. He wanted to know more of my journalistic aspirations which I had disclosed on my enlistment form. Finally, he bawled, 'Pas de journalisme ici!' and dismissed me. I was given a rail-warrant back to Paris, my days as a *légionnaire* over. I deeply regretted this, but as I later realised a full five years spent in the closed world of the Legion would have been dissatisfying. I have never lost my admiration for the Legion, or a romantic notion about what, at its best, it represents.

I thought a good deal under my bush about Indo-China, at times falling into a kind of hibernation. There was no Mekong watering the desert, but I had only to half-shut my eyes to forget my arid surroundings and be transported to the lush green panorama of Indo-China. The golden mornings, the infinite vista of rice fields, the consoling greenness of the lands of the Mekong came sharply into focus, blurring my desert surroundings, carrying me back to the adventures of the past. My nostalgic reveries also recalled the trivial things – swimming in the river, opium dreams, the scent of jasmine, and Kipling's phrase 'A neater, sweeter maiden in a cleaner, greener land'.

There I tried to come to terms with my insignificant self, seemingly forgotten beneath the stars. The memories of war were, disconcertingly, quite comforting. 'If you have survived those horrors you can survive anything,' I kept reminding myself. I thought of the harm I had done Jacqueline, and I tried to rationalise my headstrong behaviour. I climbed through the vaults of my imagination for hours each day thinking of her; she was my dream throughout my captivity. There were times under that bush when I would have given anything for her passionate embrace. I cursed the idiocy which had made me come to Ethiopia. And I wondered what the *Sunday Times* was doing about getting me out.

Then one morning, Sunday, 23 July, six weeks after my kidnapping, I listened to the BBC World Service and heard my name. With elation, I called the guerrillas over. We squatted in the sand and listened together to a crackly interview with Harold Evans, editor of the *Sunday Times*, reporting my disappearance. The broadcast proved that I had been telling the truth and from then on my captors were markedly more open and friendly.

Their positive reaction made me feel my release would come. I began counting the days, but six more weeks were to pass before I reached the Sudan – weeks of boredom and frustration, broken only when, one morning, I was taken across the sandy valley floor to another series of bushes and introduced to the Tylers, a captive English family. The Tylers had been kidnapped on 9 May, a few weeks before me, when Lindsay – a thirty-four-year-old veterinary surgeon – took his family with him on a cattle-vaccinating mission in Ethiopia's northern wilds. A blown bridge made a detour necessary and, while driving down a mountain road in the early afternoon, his Land Rover was fired on by the TPLF and forced to stop. When the news was broken to them that the guerrillas were demanding a one million dollar ransom for their release, they were exceedingly despondent. But our meeting was an exciting moment nevertheless – the only Britons for hundreds of miles brought together as captives. 'To what do we owe the pleasure . . .?' said Lindsay. Their children, Sally and Robert, jumped about and we all shook hands. Then we were allowed to eat lunch together, with the guerrillas listening all the time. They had not entirely abandoned their idea that we were members of an arcane western capitalist imperialist spy ring and were testing us, I think, to see whether we had known one another before.

In the end, I won sufficient trust to be taken on a guided tour of the impressive TPLF cave complex. Some of the caves housed hospitals and workshops and were all bustle. But one was like a grave, where Ethiopian army prisoners of war sat on their haunches in the dark, eyes sunken and melancholy, forgotten men in a forgotten place, condemned to rot for years in captivity.

Thank God, I thought (and not for the first time) that I was not born an Ethiopian. Outside, young recruits were drilling.

I was released on 6 September, thanks to the intervention of President Nimeiri of the Sudan, the BBC broadcast, and belated efforts by the *Sunday Times*. Bowing to Foreign Office advice, it had stifled any publicity about my disappearance for six weeks. This was a mistake on this occasion. The oxygen of publicity can be harmful, even dangerous in kidnapping cases; it gives the captors a misguided sense of self-importance and emboldens them to be unyielding over their demands. On the other hand, concealment of the news of a kidnapping can, as in my case, endanger the life of the victim.

When it came time to say goodbye to the Tylers I told them I would do what I could to help secure their early and safe return to Britain. During those desert days of tedium, I had watched the Tylers from my bush and grown to admire and respect the resourceful way they faced their ordeal. I had yet again the sense of being a privileged person in transit through other people's lives. In a few days I would be in Europe, while they were left to their fate. Shaking hands and saying goodbye was another act of desertion.

The Tylers were finally freed on 6 January after 238 days of captivity. Some months later, I got a letter from the TPLF's Berhu Aregawi. It said, inter alia, 'No doubt the essential part of your question has been answered. The Tylers have been set free unconditionally and unharmed. Their captivity for more than eight months is mainly due to their arrogance and the intrigue the British embassy in the Sudan tried to make. As to your release, you should be grateful only to your sincerity and integrity. Your release solely depended on your personality and job. I would like to repeat to you once more that we do not condemn kidnappings that are made for revolutionary ends.'

I was handed over unconditionally to the Sudanese police the next afternoon. For more than twelve hours we had groped our way on camel-back through the thickest sandstorm. It was the worst day I lived through in the desert. I arrived at the police station exhausted, clothes and hair gritty with sand and eyes red-rimmed from rubbing. I was taken by lorry to Port Sudan and then flown to Khartoum.

Twenty-four hours later I landed at Heathrow; sunburnt, grinning like a schoolboy, gulping in breaths of freedom. No day could have been happier. But inside there was a secret anguish.

I felt like flying out to Asia; and the sooner the better. Tomorrow, if possible, blowing my bridges behind, if necessary. But not without Jacqueline, whom I loved but whom, bizarrely and unforgivably, I had left to go to Ethiopia.

She was in the south of France. I flew to Paris and took the night train from the Gare de Lyon. The last time I had travelled on that train was as a Foreign Legion recruit running away from a *chagrin d'amour*, nervously chain-smoking *troupes* (French army cigarettes). Now I was travelling, I hoped, towards love. Raising a blind in the morning, I saw the French countryside flash by, *ravissant*, fat as butter. I had coffee and a hot croissant and for the first time in months felt I belonged among the living.

She wore a summer dress. The early sun glowed on her radiant face. She was genuinely overjoyed to see me safe. But there was something else I noticed. A distance. A mistrust. A hurt in the eyes. I saw it with a sense of foreboding. She recoiled at the unkempt figure standing before her and indeed I presented a wretched spectacle. My face was haggard, sallow-cheeked and thin. I was overcome by a great lassitude. Unknown to me, I was already suffering from hepatitis caught while a prisoner.

It was a fatal meeting, a night more of silent tears than love-making. 'If you only knew what you have done to us,' she said, 'how much of us you have destroyed.' She had believed, she said, for a long time that I was dead. There would have been a certain symmetry to my life had I died in Indo-China; she could have come to terms with that because it was the place I loved. But Ethiopia, a country so foreign to my being; to have died there would have been insane.

She did not need to say any more. I realised then that she was no longer prepared to compromise over the mad lifestyle I imposed on our relationship. Grieving for another lost journalist-lover and soul mate, after Claude Arpin, was more than her heart could bear. She had passed through enough anguish and despair and had made up her mind that they were over.

But she said she would forever wonder how I had managed so adroitly to throw away so much love. And, searching for words to reflect her feelings, she finally quoted to me a passage from *The Little Prince*: 'You know you become responsible, forever, for what you have tamed. You are responsible for your rose . . .' Jacqueline throughout those years in Indo-China was my rose; a lovely, wild, example of the exotic beauty of the lands of the Mekong. Instead of nourishing her and treating her with the tenderness she deserved; instead of staying and making her feel I was always there, I had run away. In that south of France apartment, she closed her coloured petals to me for ever. 'Tu n'as pas le coeur fidèle.' I could think of no adequate reply. The dawn and our farewells came with brutal sadness.

A disconsolate and lonely figure on the platform, the green hills behind, the blue Mediterranean in front; a circle of love that would never now be closed – that is how she vanished from my world. I left for London a free man – free but shrivelled inside, learning too late one of the most important lessons of all; that it is the time you waste for someone you love that makes them so important. I think that I had found my enemy at last: it was myself.

After the Khmer Rouge

Ethiopia was like a personal taste of hell, and when I got back to London I was more than ever convinced that the past was lost and that the future seemed hopeless. There are those who say such events make one stronger and are character-forming. That is broadly true, but I was deeply scarred by the experience of my kidnapping. This showed by the fact that in the bitter aftermath of the whole harrowing episode I was temporarily cured of my disease of restlessness to the point that I found myself doing something I had vowed I would never do – working at the London office of the *Sunday Times*. I did not become a journalist to be a journalistic bureaucrat and felt as uneasy and uncertain in that office as an immigrant does arriving in a strange land. But standing still was necessary while I sorted out what I should do next.

By and by, the old inner restlessness took hold again. I needed ripples in my life to feel alive and, looking around me in the office, it was clear I was not going to get them there. I am sure that subconsciously I was rearranging events to make the memories more palatable, for there were moments in London when I was convinced that I missed even Ethiopia and the solitude and simplicity of a captive's life in the desert. Inevitably, I went back on the road again, feeling an urgent need to be on the spot. I wandered the world in quest of news, through the carnage of Beirut, the Ogaden war, Chad, Zaire, where I renewed my acquaintance with the Foreign Legion, reporting on its second parachute regiment, the Deuxième REP, dropping onto the rebel-held town of Kolwezi.

War reporting in those early post-Vietnam war years was still like a travelling circus – the same journalistic faces I had known in Indo-China kept popping up in every conceivable trouble spot, infesting bars from Beirut to Luanda with their rich banter and performing brilliant acts of journalism like the fine bunch of 'trapeze artists' they always were. There were times, however, when I felt trapped in London and I came, quite unfairly, to regard the London office of the *Sunday Times* as a journalistic gulag. This was preposterous, for while I was prospering there, Pran, the person who more than anyone had made living possible after Cambodia, was fighting for his own survival as a prisoner in an authentic gulag – Cambodia in the Year Zero under Pol Pot, with its hopeless horror and pain.

Since that heart-rending day – 20 April 1975 – when he trudged out through the gates of the French embassy into the Cambodian countryside, there had not been an iota of news from Pran. From America, Sydney was pursuing his quest for his loyal friend as tenaciously as he had pursued the Cambodian story. Anyone, any organisation with a link with Cambodia, however tenuous, who he thought could locate Pran inside Cambodia and help him to escape, he bombarded with relentless requests for help and information.

How many times had I thought of Pran as I shuttled around the world's trouble-spots? Not often enough, I confess. It was not insensitivity, I hope; more that I had unconsciously allowed a gulf to develop between me and Indo-China for my own protection and sanity in the new present. And there was also a big residue of guilt. I and other westerners had saved our skins while Pran and other Cambodians to whom we owed debts of loyalty had been imprisoned or killed. How did we square that one? I, for instance, had not only survived; I had flourished to the point where I now had a staff job on a leading Sunday newspaper.

One overcast autumn day, I was standing in the foreign department of the old offices in Gray's Inn Road, thinking about nothing in particular, when the telex machine chattered into life. It was a message addressed to me from Sydney in Bangkok, telling me that Pran was safe. At the end of it was a personal, cosmic message from Pran, patterned after a Cambodian proverb. 'Hi Jon. The world is round. Now I meet you again. Pran was in bad shape, but the life is remained. Love Pran.'

I held the flimsy telex message in my hand and stared out of the window in disbelief, beyond the blackened roof-tops and the construction cranes to a distant blue patch of sky as if it were the sunshine lighting up Southeast Asia. The present melted away and I saw Phnom Penh again – the familiar streets, the triumphant beauty of the Mekong in full flood, the rice paddies, the majestic sadness of a tortured but beautiful land. So Pran had survived, limping out of Cambodia into a refugee camp in Thailand. Life had an extra special meaning that day.

Pran's escape marked the end of a four-year nightmare for Sydney. Tortured by Pran's disappearance, he had led an uncompromising one-man crusade to trace his helper and friend who had so courageously saved our lives. 'This is the most wonderful, wonderful news. Please give Pran my love and a big hug from someone who owes him everything,' I said in a cable to Sydney, who had flown to Thailand to welcome Pran. It was the best news out of Indo-China for a long while.

Pran's survival was a triumph of self-reliance, of tenacity, of endurance over an insanely brutal regime. Toiling in Pol Pot's gulag, he had never given up hope that Sydney would find a way to rescue him; but the magnificent thing was that his escape was authentically his own doing. His powerful American friends with all their good intentions, their dollars and the resources at their disposal could do nothing for him in the end. A Cambodian had stood upon his own feet, demonstrating that Cambodians could be their own masters whatever cruel lessons to the contrary the war had taught. As Warren Hoffecker, an American working with refugees in Thailand, said in a letter to Sydney, 'the era of American miracles is over . . . and there is nothing you can do.'

On leaving the French embassy, Pran had even thrown away the thousands of US dollars Sydney had given him in case they compromised him. He had made his way through the chaos of millions of people on the move, to his native province of Siem Reap. There he joined a work gang in the fields. He soon realised that the Khmer Rouge were rooting out and killing people with education or past links with foreigners, and he hoodwinked them into thinking he was just an ignorant taxi-driver. Several times, he came within an inch of his life, but he survived, living off his wits, often with nothing more to eat than ants and bugs. He bided his time and finally on 3 October 1979 – 1627 days after we had abandoned him – he crossed the border to Thailand and safety.

His trek to freedom took him through the Khmer Rouge execution grounds – the Killing Fields – burial pits littered with the remains of thousands of Cambodians axed and clubbed to death. He set out for the border with eleven other Cambodians. The fugitives had to move through the jungle stealthily, in single file, avoiding random Khmer Rouge patrols, booby traps and unmarked minefields. The last part of the journey was only sixty miles, but it took seventeen days. The final cruelty was that they had almost reached the border when a mine blew the two young men immediately in front of Pran to bits. He was lightly grazed by shrapnel. When he emerged, his health was breaking down – his teeth were falling out; he was suffering from malaria. Most of his family had died under Pol Pot; but he at least was safe and his escape from that death-haunted land helped to relieve our guilt.

It was time now for me to go back to Cambodia and see what had happened to the country I loved. Nearly five years had passed since the fall of Phnom Penh and Cambodia was dogged, once again, by civil war and was emerging from a terrible famine. A new government was in power in Phnom Penh, installed by the communist Vietnamese who had invaded a year previously and set up a pro-Vietnamese communist state under Hanoi's discreet direction. Using the Khmer Rouge massacre of thousands of Vietnamese villagers on the border as justification, their tanks and columns had moved up Highway One, crossed the Mekong at Neak Leung and, in a five-day blitzkrieg, rumbled into Phnom Penh and put the Khmer Rouge to flight. The population was too enfeebled by the demagogic exigencies of the Khmer Rouge tyranny to meet the Vietnamese with any effective resistance; the country was quickly overrun and Pol

247

Pot chased to the border with Thailand, where he remains to this day.

If the Vietnamese had not attacked when they did, Cambodia might not have survived much longer. All that Pol Pot left behind was blood and ruins. His dream of raising a new Khmer civilisation, greater even than the Angkorian era, had turned people into a race of human ants, toiling for long hours in rural rice communes on starvation rations of rice gruel, under the guns of young, hostile Khmer Rouge guards.

Now the whole nation was on the move again, as people returned to their homes, searched for their loved ones, tried to rebuild their lives. But Cambodia was still closed to the world. Helped by the indefatigable Guy Stringer, deputy director of Oxfam, who bust through red tape to get the first western aid into Phnom Penh, and Chum Bun Rong, a gendarmerie lieutenant whom I had known slightly in the Lon Nol times and who had miraculously survived and was working in the information department of the new foreign ministry, I was granted a visa.

On New Year's Day 1980, I took off from Bangkok on an International Red Cross flight for Phnom Penh, one of the first British journalists to be allowed in. In normal times, it was a one-hour flight, but the Vietnamese authorities perversely obliged our French air force Transall to fly a dogleg route, out to sea, then over Saigon, and finally into Phnom Penh.

I think I felt more emotional crossing the Vietnamese coast and passing directly above Saigon, where every detail of that dear city was uncannily visible, than landing in Phnom Penh again. Britain had already been alerted to the horrors of the Khmer Rouge regime, notably by *Year Zero*, a shaming television documentary made by

John Pilger and David Munro, which had elicited a fantastic public response; yet I was not ready for the shock of coming back.

The sense of homecoming I felt as I drove into the city from the airport did not last long. There was an overwhelming sense of emptiness and I was frightened by what I would find. I was staying in the Monorom, one of two hotels to be reopened; the other was my old stamping ground, the Hôtel Le Phnom, which had now been taken over by the international aid agencies.

The first thing I did on that first day was to walk down the street to the Phnom, now renamed the Samaki or Solidarity Hotel, a new buzzword to emphasise the friendship between the Cambodian and Vietnamese people. I passed the empty ground where the Roman Catholic cathedral blown up by the Khmer Rouge had stood; not a brick of the building remained. I passed the old Air France office where so many frightened people had queued for tickets out to Bangkok, Singapore and Paris in the last days of the siege of Phnom Penh. I passed the former press centre where Am Rong delivered his surreal briefings, the Lycée Descartes, and through the gates to the hotel which had for months been home. It was in poor state, its garden weed-grown, its pool filled with stagnant water; I looked in something of a daze at the studio where I had lived, now occupied by a Swiss aid worker.

Many times in the past four and a half years, I had been stabbed with nostalgia and regret. Now I was here at last. I sat at the little bar drinking a glass of imported beer. The heat and the unhurried pace of life suggested nothing had changed. The beer was cold, and the girl who served it was soft and pretty and spoke French. The ceiling fan whirred gently. The same faded photographs of the Angkor temples hung on the walls. With eyes half-closed and senses lulled by the tinkle of a gamelan in the background, it seemed for a moment as though I had never left.

I was jolted sharply out of this reverie: Sitha, the girl behind the counter, suddenly began to weep. Soon she was pouring out the story of her exodus from Phnom Penh, the destruction of her family. Her sorrow made me feel awkward and clumsy. A couple of the old hotel staff who had survived also came in, their hair white and eyes sunken – older, thinner, sadder. One by one, they shook my hand, embarrassed. I was equally embarrassed, at a loss for words, and could only hold their hands affectionately, give them a hug, and clumsily hand them some money, then turn away. They all wanted to know what had happened to Monsieur Loup, the old proprietor, who had been evacuated to France, but I could not help them. My hold on reality was slipping.

For hours, I walked the streets as if in a spell, looking at the city. The bonds were not broken, but they were fraying. The sense of belonging was missing. The golden past could not be reborn. The magic was going. Nothing, it seemed, was left; nothing at all. The two Phnom Penhs were separated by a few years in time but for ever in mood. Around me was a wasteland of decaying and melancholy buildings and a distraught and traumatised people, desperately trying to rebuild their lives. Phnom Penh had visibly contracted; there was sadness in every face. But none of the faces I saw was familiar; they were all new people. After the Vietnamese invasion had freed them from the tyranny of Pol Pot, they had rushed into Phnom Penh from the countryside and moved into whatever home they could grab. Most had no concept of living in an urban community.

The moment I stepped off the main boulevards I entered another, subterranean world, like passing from sunlight to darkness. These side streets had once been frantic places, and now they were the graveyards of the modern civilisation, as it had existed before the Khmer Rouge had rejected it. Rusting cars, lorries, buses and refrigerators lay among the stinking piles of refuse. Many of the old traditional houses, with their great wooden floors and their carved roofs, had been torn down in a frenzy of destruction, as symbols of the *petite bourgeoisie*. Everywhere there were swarms of flies, the smell of decay; and pigs, dogs and chickens were rooting in the dirt.

In the city centre, not a single shop was functioning or open; the cavernous market was deserted. The interiors of many houses had been looted. The pavements and drains were broken. Hopeless groups of people crouched on the pavements and against the walls, bartering for a few handfuls of rice, suffering etched on their faces. In places, people with rickety limbs moved like zombies searching for their loved ones or scraps of food. It was nothing to duck into the doorway of a hut and be confronted by diseased and malnourished children, flyblown or with eyes glazed over by approaching death. Among the shapeless bundles outside Phnom Penh railway station was a woman clasping a new-born baby, which was dying, and a brace of orphans whining in hunger. How that faint sound of whining carried in the wind and penetrated my ears.

Clearly, not much had improved in the year since the Vietnamese army had first rolled into Phnom Penh and found it silent and deserted; the central bank blown up, its banknotes – now worthless

– scattered everywhere, the colonnaded shops and villas looted and smashed, the factories at a standstill, the streets knee-deep in broken furniture and rubble. Unless one was there, one could not realise how desperate it was. In Phnom Penh at this time, there was still no paper to write on and few pens to write with. The ministries, such as they were, had hardly a typewriter among them and almost no means of copying a document. There were no telephones to make appointments. There was no proper postal system. Letters for the provinces were carried by truck drivers travelling upcountry. There had been no money since the Khmer Rouge abolished the currency. Those who had a second shirt or sarong, even a second pair of sandals, were lucky. The Monorom Hotel had no knives and forks and so could not serve even breakfast; I was asked to bring some cutlery from Bangkok on my next visit, so that they could open a restaurant for us. All had been destroyed; an entire country had to be rebuilt.

I poked around in the old British embassy, where several families were squatting amid the wrecked filing cabinets. Someone had been digging up the garden – looking for buried money and jewellery, my guide suggested – though why there should be any hidden there, I could not imagine. The Khmer Rouge had burned the books. I went back to the Bibliothèque Nationale, next to the Hôtel Le Phnom, which had opened its doors a few days previously, following a closure which had lasted nearly five years. It was a distressing sight. Once, it had been full of beautiful books about the antiquity of Cambodia. These had all been destroyed, but the English novel was represented by two books – George Orwell's *Burmese Days* and *Little Women* – incongruously together on the shelf. There were no monks.

The pagodas were empty. This was the joyless Phnom Penh I had come back to.

A couple of days later, I found my first real friend from the past. I found So Pheap. I was walking down a street near the post office and a woman in ragged black pyjamas stopped her bicycle in front of me and said shyly, 'Jon, is it you?' As I nodded and rushed over, I detected in her sad face a silent reproach. The Khmer Rouge had turned So Pheap from a delicate copper-skinned beauty into a rough peasant girl. Her hair was clipped short, her skin had coarsened in the sun, her rubber-sandalled feet were torn and her beautiful hands covered in sores. She was ringed by sorrow and quivered with emotion.

'Maman morte, bébé morte,' she said, with a look of utter sadness. We arranged to meet later that evening outside the hotel. I hoped to be able to give her some money. But then my interpreter appeared, and she stiffened, gave me a last imploring glance and cycled away, terrified she would be denounced to the communist authorities for addressing a westerner. And though I searched and searched the streets of Phnom Penh for days afterwards, I never found her again. Another door closed on the past for ever.

Chantal's *fumerie* was now in a Vietnamese army special security zone fenced off with barbed wire. My efforts to visit it were firmly rebuffed by a hawk-faced sentry. Nothing could be done and I did not insist. In the street behind it was Tuol Sleng, the *lycée* which the Khmer Rouge had operated as an extermination camp. Its doors had been a portal of death for 16,000 murdered people. In past days, when it was a *lycée*, I had often glided by in a cyclo on my way to sneak a quiet afternoon's *pipe* at Chantal's, and I remembered the girls and boys with their satchels of books, sauntering down the rough road in the sunshine on their way home at the end of a school day.

I spent many bleak hours inside Tuol Sleng, now converted into a museum by the Vietnamese to justify their invasion and overthrow of Pol Pot. But the vision of evil lingers in my mind: classrooms divided into tiny brick cells where prisoners were held in solitary confinement; each interrogation room equipped with an iron bed, to which they were chained, naked, with iron shackles; a desk and a chair provided for the interrogator; gallows outside to suspend the prisoners by their feet; stone vats of water into which they were plunged head first. The prison was ringed by a double fence of barbed wire – a needless precaution; nobody escaped.

In the cells, the invading Vietnamese had found the rotting remains of fourteen tortured prisoners. A year later, brown blotches of blood still stained the floor; decaying mounds of evil-smelling clothing stripped off the victims by the guards revealed the human agony of this dark place.

Like the Nazis, the Khmer Rouge had a mania for documenting their deeds; every prisoner who entered Tuol Sleng was photographed and forced to write a confession to which he attached a thumbprint and signature. The Vietnamese had recovered the documentation, developed the films and displayed the pictures all in one room: row upon row of photos of guards, blank-faced, idiotic, cruel, ugly – and on the opposite walls, the photos of their victims, agony and terror on their faces as they awaited the end. Standing in the semi-obscurity of this cold, still room looking at the wall-to-wall images, I could hear the screams of the tortured, imagine the breaking flesh.

One of the photographs was of the camp guards, their wives and

children, all in black garb. In the middle of the back row, distinct
with his preposterous protruding ears, was Kang Kek Ieu, alias
Comrade Deuch, the prison director. Comrade Deuch was the very
same Khmer Rouge cadre who had interrogated my friend François
Bizot during his captivity near Oudong in 1971. Now he had turned
up here in a photo like a bad penny. Deuch's signature was found
repeatedly on the death warrants. In one, I saw he had ordered the
purging of an entire Khmer Rouge battalion, including two nine-
year-old soldiers, because it was thought disloyal. 'Kill them all,' he
wrote above his nightmare squiggle and the date.

Deuch's interrogators delighted in their work. The ingenuity of
their methods of torture chills the mind. Confessions were extracted
by means of whips, chains, water baths and poisonous reptiles. Many
of the prisoners were ranking Khmer Rouge cadres; as the regime
devoured its own, they were executed as spies and traitors.

One of the victims was Hu Nim, the Khmer Rouge's Information
Minister. He had been one of the earliest revolutionaries, a top
leader and confidant of Pol Pot; he was accused by his comrades of
collaboration with the Vietnamese and of having CIA connections.
Sent to Tuol Sleng on 10 April 1977, he was tortured. After four
days, a first pathetic confession by Hu Nim was handed to Deuch
by Pon, his interrogator. A note was attached: 'We whipped him
four or five times to break his stand, before taking him to be stuffed
with water.' Eight days later, Pon reported back to Deuch: 'I have
tortured him to write it again.' On 6 July, Hu Nim was executed.

I felt indifferent to his suffering and death. He was not a victim
in the way the others were victims. He was now on the receiving
end of what his terrible organisation had done to thousands upon
thousands of ordinary Cambodians. I got a grim satisfaction from

the realisation that there was retributive justice in Cambodia after all. He did not deserve human pity.

The pictures of the other victims are blurred in my mind, but I still see one – a big black-and-white blow-up of Hu Nim's wife, a single tear glistening and rolling down her cheek, her eyes bulging in white terror. It was impossible not to be moved by that image. But there was no reason for sorrow. As the wife of this top-ranking Khmer Rouge official, Madame Hu Nim had some responsibility for what happened. I had no sympathy for her.

Several westerners were also tortured and killed at Tuol Sleng: carefree young drifters sailing aimlessly through the waves of Southeast Asia on holidays of a lifetime, one day they strayed too close in their yachts to the Cambodian coast and were captured by Khmer Rouge gunboats. I wondered a lot about that moment of capture. There had been nothing in their lives of idle pleasure and youthful irresponsibility to prepare them for the terrors in store. As the black-clad soldiers boarded, they could not have imagined that they were going to be taken to an extermination camp and tortured to death. Each was accused of spying against Cambodia and was forced, under torture, to make a detailed confession of CIA involvement and training. Copies of their confessions, extracted by the cruellest tortures, were afterwards found in the prison camp. The statements of two French brothers, twenty-two and twenty-six when they were killed, just echoed puzzlement and stupefaction: '. . . ne sachant rien de la cause de notre arrêt . . . je ne sais pas du tout la faute que j'ai commis,' one wrote.

The confessions of other foreigners were more revealing. In a desperate attempt to satisfy the spy hysteria of their torturers and save their skins, they fabricated CIA activities for themselves, weaving them into real events in their lives. In his 4000 word confession, Kerry Hamill, a New Zealander, claimed he was recruited into the agency by his father, supposedly a CIA colonel. He described, in considerable detail, the agency's plans to subvert the Khmer Rouge regime. James Clarke and Christopher Lance, both Americans, and Ron Dean and David Scott, Australians, gave equally imaginative and fictitious accounts of their espionage activities in Asia. Dean's yacht, the fifty-two-foot ketch *Sanuk*, had been captured on 2 November 1978, while on its way to a Thai port to have a new teak deck fitted. He signed his confession on 21 November, after nearly three weeks of whippings, the bastinado (caning of the soles of the feet) and electric shocks to the genitals. By the time the Vietnamese reached Tuol Sleng six weeks later, he and the other westerners had been savagely murdered. They were repeatedly hanged by the feet, let down into a vat of water and hanged again, to die at last of strangulation. All that Deuch needed to justify having them killed in this inhumane manner was their signatures and thumbprint on their confessions, to show that he had caught a group of 'imperialist spies'.

Also found at Tuol Sleng were the nine rules of conduct Deuch made his foreign prisoners obey while undergoing torture.

Regulations of Security Agents

1. You must answer in conformity with the questions I asked you. Don't try and turn away my questions.
2. Don't try to escape by making pretexts according to your hypocritical ideas. It is strictly forbidden to contest me.
3. Don't be a fool for you are a chap who dare to thwart the revolution.

257

4. You must immediately answer my questions without wasting the time to reflect.

5. Don't tell me about your little incidents committed against the propriety. Don't tell me either about the essence of the revolution.

6. During the bastinado or the electrization [sic] you must not cry loudly.

7. Do sit down quietly. Wait for the orders. If there are no orders, do nothing. If I ask you to do something, you must immediately do it without protesting.

8. Don't make pretexts about Kampuchea-Krom in order to hide your jaw of traitor.

9. If you disobey every point of my regulations you will get either ten strokes of whip or five shock of electric discharge.

What kind of man was the mass killer who ordered his men to carry out such hideous tortures? I was determined to find out, but none of my Cambodian friends could enlighten me; Ing Pech, one of the only known Tuol Sleng survivors – he got away the day after the Vietnamese captured the city on 7 January 1979 – was not forthcoming either. He said that as the director of the prison, Deuch had lived a life of relative affluence in a comfortably furnished house nearby which now served as the Polish embassy. He visited the prison regularly, sometimes with his wife in tow. 'He had a kind and gentle manner, but everyone was terrified of him,' Pech said. 'His favourite expression was "This man is bad and needs to be re-educated." When you heard that you knew Deuch meant tortured and killed.'

Deuch escaped. As the Vietnamese fought their way into the

suburbs of Phnom Penh, he fled with hundreds of other Khmer Rouge officials to the Thai border. To the embarrassment of western refugee officials, he crossed into Thailand and hid in a Khmer Rouge refugee camp which was receiving food and medical aid from the international relief agencies. After three months, he crossed back into Cambodia and rejoined Pol Pot's forces in the west of the country, to fight the Vietnamese.

I could find no one in Phnom Penh who knew about Deuch's early life. But his parents were still alive and inside Cambodia. Later on, I tried to trace them, travelling up to the district town of Strung, in Kompong Thom province. The journey was the first westerners had been permitted to that part of Cambodia, Pol Pot's birthplace, and the area was still insecure. As we rattled through the countryside, around the Great Lake, past Angkor and Kompong Thom, the country was as I remembered; an unforgettable composition of inundated rice fields, palm trees and misty hills.

Here and there, giant canals cut through the landscape. They had been feverishly dug with bare hands under the eyes of vengeful Khmer Rouge guards. Most had now been abandoned as useless. I was appalled by the destruction and continuing misery; people were still living off leaves. In the remotest places we visited, there was latent hostility, either because we were foreigners or because we had come from the city. We were driving along a lonely stretch of road at dusk, about to cross a bridge, when we were challenged by a group of government soldiers. They were scowling peasant boys, dark-skinned forest people, probably defectors from the Khmer Rouge. Tense minutes followed as they surrounded our car and poked rifles through the windows. Eventually, they let us pass for double the usual number of bribes of cigarettes. Our government 'minder' was trembling with fright.

At Strung, I found a watery eyed old woman with black-lacquered teeth, and her husband, parents of the mass-murderer, living in a large, spacious teak house on stilts, where Deuch had grown up. It was clear that his mother had no idea what a monster her son had become. I could not bring myself to tell her as we sat on the floor and sipped bitter Chinese tea. I did not want to burden an already old and troubled mind. She spoke of Deuch with a mother's love. 'He was a good, respectful boy who helped his parents.' Her husband, a half-Chinese fisherman with a mouthful of gold teeth, said his son had studied hard and had come top of the class. 'He was something of a loner,' the old woman conceded. 'He read a lot and seldom played with the other children in the village.'

She had seen him only once in recent years. One day after the Khmer Rouge victory, he drove up in a car with a military escort and announced his forthcoming marriage. He ordered his mother to accompany him to Phnom Penh. She had never before been to the big city, one hundred miles away, and was flattered at the invitation. But Deuch did not allow her to stay. She was driven back to Strung after the wedding. She had not seen Deuch again. The journey had made her realise that her son had an important role in the Khmer Rouge. Why then, she wondered, were no special privileges accorded her husband and herself? They had suffered like the rest of the population and hated the Khmer Rouge. It was a sad, unsatisfactory meeting. I came away unable to put a human face to Deuch's evil. Indisputably he was fanatical and cruel, a man who listened to no plea for mercy; yet many of his victims were from among his own kind. Perhaps there is a clue in the fact that he spent three years in

260

a political jail under Prince Sihanouk. Deuch's mother assumed her son had been tortured in jail, so perhaps he was taking revenge for his suffering. On his release he had gone underground and joined Pol Pot.

When I got back to Phnom Penh, I went around the old French embassy, now a Vietnamese army camp. Partly in ruins and stinking of human excrement, the walls were covered in soldiers' graffiti. Not a trace remained of our time there. A host of memories passed before my eyes: soldiers rotting at the wayside; the white knuckles of a woman's hand clenching the child torn from her grasp; burial pits of skulls polished like billiard balls; pitiful fragments of bodies carried from the battlefields; the corruption, the incompetence, the intrigue, the dust, the soldiers, the refugees, the war without end. Cambodia at its worst was truly ugly.

I stood still by the broken span of the bridge across one of the *quatre bras* of the Mekong, where the Khmer Rouge had been going to execute us. My mood was melancholy, filled with wistful regret. I thought of the lost ideals, the unfulfilled expectations, the changes that inevitably come in the course of a man's life. Was the original man who had stood at this spot, a gun pointed at his head, still alive? I wondered. Or had he perished with his beliefs as surely as if a bullet had been fired from that gun and shattered his skull that day?

261

Before me was the Mekong, immense, unchangeable, sweeping past on its eternal journey to the South China Sea; and, contemplating it for the first time since my return to Phnom Penh, I felt a link with my past. The Mekong was the river of my youth. My eyes caught the golden glitter of sunlight vibrating on its rumpled waters; my melancholy mood dissolved into the promise of better days to come, and my spirits sang.

Adieu l'Indochine

Like dreams
carved from bars
of ivory soap
you float by and melt away
with the passing of each day,
growing smaller
and smaller
until there is nothing
left of you
to touch . . .

My memories of Saigon lay for many years beneath the surface, too painful to bring out into the open again. The idea of going back filled me with dread, and whenever I thought of arranging a visit something got in the way; most often my own doubts and fears. It was not until ten years after the city's fall that I felt I had gathered the strength to return. Even then I boarded the Air France flight to Vietnam with a strange, taut feeling in my stomach.

My trepidation grew as we crossed the Vietnamese coast: down there was the Mekong, the fields of rice, the buffalo browsing in their pools, the eternal bomb craters. After a long downward glide, we landed at Tan Son Nhut airport and as we taxied, I stared in silence through the oval window, taking it all in. The rows and rows of curved hangars, divided by concrete blast walls, which once had housed the might of the US air force, were still intact; only now they were empty. A scrapheap of American aircraft and helicopters, bare and stripped hulks, slumbered at the far end of the base.

At its peak, this had been the busiest airport in the world, where passenger airliners shared the runway with fighter-bombers and lumbering military transport planes filled with troops and ammunition. Now that madness had all dissipated together with the constant noise; the guard towers; the mess halls; the storage depots; the GIs on fork-lift trucks, sweating in the heat, loading and unloading war supplies. There were miles and miles of empty runways and a few Vietnamese soldiers in olive-green uniforms and pith helmets, standing desultorily in the sunshine, smoking cigarettes. The emptiness and heavy stillness was devastating.

There was almost no motor traffic in the sunstruck streets. The blue-and-yellow taxis had gone, replaced by a few Soviet Volgas and Japanese vans. Motor bikes, bicycles and cyclos rattled by. My car slid past the twin-spired Cathedral of Our Lady and turned into Tu Do, the main street, which seemed to have shrunk, like the buildings.

But looking down a few hours later from my hotel window on what the communists had renamed Ho Chi Minh city, I found, with a lurch of recognition, that I could easily bring back the Saigon of the war: the sluggish brown river clogged with rusting hulks, the pollution and roar of the Hondas, the whining beggars, stray children, pimps and flirtatious girls.

Saigon had been a city of wild excesses; a bloated booming Sin City, dubbed the biggest whorehouse on earth; a city of slums made from plywood, cardboard and flattened tin cans, where garbage flowed onto the streets; an ugly city of barbed wire, guns and sandbags, always on the edge of catastrophe; a city of depravity; the Sodom of the East.

I echo all the familiar complaints. But to those of us who were captivated by it, Saigon was a poignant city which aroused powerful human emotions. It was often a cruel and unkind place. Who could fail to be moved by the poverty and the distress of the orphans and waifs, the dust of life? But it was a city, too, of love and spontaneous friendships and of brave people who tried with honesty and dignity

266

to lead good lives despite the war. Many of them I counted among my friends.

Swarms of lively, eager-faced children descended on me, tugging at my pocket and heart strings. I looked eagerly for the places I remembered: Chez Henri, the Club Nautique, the bar in Tu Do where Graham Greene had a girl; the Phu To race-track where the Viet Cong once controlled the back-strait. They had become as nothing. The Hôtel Royal was now a textile warehouse. The Cercle Sportif was lifeless, the paint peeling. The clubhouse was boarded up and the swimming pool drained of water. Grass sprouted between cracks in the concrete. It was all shabby, rundown, sad. But I felt sure that Saigon would rise from the ashes of the war. Down by the river front where in *The Quiet American* the fictional Fowler had watched American war planes being disembarked there were cargo ships from many nations.

I went back to my old flat. Were Monsieur Ottavj's opium pipes still behind the wardrobe where I had hidden them all those years before? It was important to know. The building was now a billet for officers of the Vietnamese army. Would they permit me to have a look? I opened the door to be met by a sullen soldier. Instinctively I froze. My reflexes were ill-attuned to the sight of a man in a North Vietnamese army uniform standing inside my old apartment building. Throwing me a suspicious glance, he signalled me to leave.

Giant billboards everywhere proclaimed that this was the anniversary of the Liberation. Unsurprisingly, the ideology of Mac-Lenin, as the Vietnamese translated Marxism-Leninism, had failed to take root in Saigon despite the arrival from Hanoi of serried ranks of tough northern cadres dedicated to instilling party discipline.

The communists had almost cut the heart out of the city; almost, but not quite. Saigon was still stubbornly insubordinate, a city of whispers, intrigue and defiance. Somewhere here were the underground escape networks that had organised the flight of boat people from Vietnam.

One day I met Kim again, a girl from one of the gentlest and noblest of Vietnamese families; a family with an abiding honesty which looked with disgust and almost with shame at the destruction the American military presence had wrought on civilised Vietnamese values and had kept their heads upright through those corrupt days. She was a friend from the war. In 1975, the communists had brutally confiscated her parents' beautiful house, compelling them to live modestly in a poor suburb. They adapted to their impoverished circumstances with characteristic dignity and good manners.

We sat in a coffee shop in the city centre. She was wearing a silk *aó dài*, a slim attentive and cultured woman with long jet-black hair, speaking faultless French and English. She kept looking nervously about her; to be seen talking to a foreigner was possibly dangerous. We sat there chatting for perhaps thirty minutes. Then, for no apparent reason, tears streamed down her face. She pulled herself together and with downcast eyes told me that for the past ten years she had been too traumatised to set foot in the centre of the town where her old home stood, or put on an *aó dài*; she did not want to be reminded of the happiness which had died on the day of 'liberation', the day the communists took power, the day they won the war. Like many other Saigonese she had always visualised that day – the first day of peace – as being the best of her life. For Kim it was the beginning of a nightmare.

She had been accused of being a spy (and was still under a small cloud) because, almost on the eve of the city's capture, she had cut short her studies in Australia to come back to Saigon. She had come back because she was a Vietnamese who loved her country, believed in its traditions and wanted to be there to give support to her parents at this critical time. It was an emotion the communists did not understand. Her life was blighted.

Another friend I met was Tuan, a Vietnamese who had worked as a freelance combat photographer for Agence France-Presse. He, too, regretted staying behind and told me that even ten years afterwards the authorities still frowned on contact with foreigners. Typing in his home late one night, he found the building surrounded by security police with detection equipment. A neighbour had mistaken his typing for the tapping of a message in Morse code and was convinced a CIA spy was operating from the building.

At the press conference celebrating the anniversary, the pat answers of the communist cadres that all was sweetness and light plainly were not true. Megaphones blared propaganda. The stage management of the event was flagrant. Beneath the surface of bustle and excitement, there was agony. The discrepancy between those in power and those subjected to the system was glaring. Most people were struggling to survive. Bug-eyed children, squatting on the pavement, sold bottles of petrol next to a stall which offered half a dozen different brands of fine cognac. Making ends meet was as much a hustle as it had ever been. The contents of entire households were up for sale in the shops. Saddest of all were the cripples, the former ARVN soldiers made outcasts by the regime. Seeing these defeated men scrabbling on their crutches outside hotels and restaurants for a few scraps of charity, reminded me that many ARVN units had been brave fighters.

I remembered the colonel in the defeated Saigon army who

269

marched in full uniform up to the war memorial in the city centre on the day of Saigon's fall, stood rigidly to attention, saluted and shot himself in the head. Now the memorial has disappeared – blown up by the communists. I did not see a re-education camp. But my colleagues told me about their visit to one in North Vietnam – a bleak and dreary place set up to reform and remould senior officers of the South Vietnamese army. They had been released, but a particular commander was still in detention because of his stubborn refusal to knuckle under. He recognised the journalist Neil Davis the instant he walked in. Forbidden by the guards to talk, he closed and opened his eyes swiftly as a sign of acknowledgement. Then he smiled at Davis through the tears.

As I wandered the streets, thoughts of the past obsessed me. Finally, by myself, I went back to Thai Lap Thanh, where Jacqueline had lived. A quiver of recognition ran down my spine as I turned the corner, past a gaggle of screeching children playing with a dead rat. I half-imagined it would no longer exist, but the little house was there, a faded sign above the iron grille of the door saying 'dressmaker'. It was now a café and noodle shop. I stood across the street and watched the people sitting at the tables, smiling and laughing, the privileged grown-up children of communist cadres from Hanoi who had appropriated her house.

I sat on a tiny stool and ordered a *café*. I tried hard to swallow it but something rose in my throat. I asked one of the children playing if she knew who had lived in the house before. She shook her head. 'Are you a stranger in Saigon?' she asked. 'I used to live here,' I said.

I got up and walked inside the café. Suddenly I was aware of two big shining green eyes – a black and white cat lying in the sun outside. With a thud of the heart, I recognised that it was Slap, Jacqueline's kitten, born in war, still alive in a Saigon at peace. The communist upheaval had left the cat untouched while it had destroyed the lives of the people around it. I went over to stroke it. With a start, it was up and bounding away. It was still the master of its own life, unlike so many of us whose lives had come to a full stop here. I turned and walked away from the street for ever.

Epilogue

I was in Indo-China for only five years. But I know that in my heart I will be there all my life. I will always lament its romantic past and sentimentalise the grand adventure of death we lived through in the midst of such ravishing beauty. Perhaps I am deceived by unworldly dreams. Perhaps I weave too many illusions about the past. But I don't believe it was just a romantic fantasy. After years of travel, I have encountered nowhere like Indo-China, and I am not alone in this. Whole generations of westerners who went out there as soldiers, doctors, planters or journalists like myself, to document the sorrow, the tragedy and the stories of its wars, lost their hearts to these lands of the Mekong. They are places that take over a man's soul. The pain of memory endures alongside this nostalgia. Some memories remained buried in a body bag so deep within me that it was years before I let them out.

Vietnam is part of history now. It is more than twenty years since the last American combatants left; more than forty since the French army's defeat at Dien Bien Phu. In Washington, more than 58,000 names of Americans killed in Indo-China are sand-blasted into the granite of the Vietnam Veterans' Memorial, mourned by their comrades-in-arms and by their families. Their sacrifices in a war that split America still weigh heavily on the nation's psyche. In Vietnam, the United States had experienced defeat for the first time in its history and that defeat has altered international perceptions of it as a superpower. It has raised doubts, still present in America, about whether the United States should fight a foreign war again.

At last the French, too, have been able to honour their Indo-China war dead, erecting a memorial at Dien Bien Phu in honour of all those who died for France. For his part, General Marcel Bigeard, one of the indomitable paratroop commanders of that battle, whose heroic stand against overwhelming odds set the highest standards of professional soldiering, has expressed the wish for his ashes, when he comes to make his 'grand saut dans l'inconnu', to be dropped by parachute over the battlefield; to mingle with the ravaged earth where his comrades fell. 'C'est bien en Indochine que j'ai laissé la moitié de mon coeur,' he said.

Countless thousands of Vietnamese, Cambodians and Laotians, who fought as soldiers on all sides, or were civilians caught up in the fighting, have no proper resting place and little recognition that their suffering mattered. This is true above all for the ex-ARVN who fought on the South Vietnamese side. In the sentiment of Nguyen Du, the eighteenth-century Vietnamese poet, they are the Wandering Souls searching for peace.

Meanwhile, the small struggling nations of Indo-China continue the quest for lasting peace, proper international recognition, and the regeneration of their countries against hard odds. In the second half

276

of the twentieth century, they endured the worst extremes of human suffering. The story is by no means over yet. Each day that passes sees a fresh crop of injuries from the millions of unexploded mines, shells and American bombs littering jungles and rice fields, especially in Laos and Cambodia.

Journalism, too, had its casualties in Indo-China, as this book relates. The figures are still being assessed. But according to the research of the Indo-China Media Memorial Foundation, 320 journalists of all nations did not return. And one or two tragically became casualties of the war long after the bullets ceased to fly; unable to cope with the difficult transition to peacetime living, they killed themselves.

Indo-China cast a potent spell over many of those it touched. Nothing has been able to break that spell for my friend Bizot, either; not the passage of the years, nor even the closeness of his family. The Frenchman persists in thinking about it every day. He has taken away and stored the gates of the old French embassy in Phnom Penh because he feels they ought to be preserved. The great wrought-iron gates were a witness to the city's fall; and it is right that they should have been rescued, above all by Bizot who was their guardian during the dark days when they and his matter-of-fact heroism were all that stood between us and the murderous Khmer Rouge; not destroyed, as they were otherwise inevitably destined to be, in the redevelopment of the old embassy ruins.

Bizot's own story of his captivity by the Khmer Rouge in 1971 inspired John Le Carré to write a poignant short story; I think it is the best to be found in his book *The Secret Pilgrim*. As for the little Khmer Rouge girl who used to check the ropes binding his ankles and have them tightened if they were loose, the memory of her eyes have never left the Frenchman. Perhaps sometimes he sees them superimposed on the eyes of his daughter Hélène; she who was so much in his mind's eye during those three months in captivity.

On an impulse, Hélène, ignorant of the country of her birth because she grew up in France, gave up a modelling career in Paris and New York to go back to Cambodia. It was a pilgrimage to uncover her roots. The unrivalled corruption and greed of the new Cambodia marred the experience, and soon she left in despair and disillusionment. If only she had been able to see what her father had seen, she would have loved Cambodia more than enough.

When I last saw Bizot, after we had lost sight of each other for many, many years, he told me that he had dreamed that I had died in the Middle East. It was while I was a captive in Ethiopia; it was a prescient dream. For years afterwards, he said, he believed I was dead. 'It's a lucky sign,' he said. He also echoed Jacqueline's reaction, saying that if I was doomed to die, then to perish anywhere other than in the lands of the Mekong would have been tragic injustice.

Today, Bizot lives with his beautiful new family in Chiang Mai, in northern Thailand. He lives his own life in a magnificent teak house on stilts, which he built as the Southeast Asia headquarters of the École Française d'Extrème Orient, and works on his Buddhist texts and manuscripts with as much diligence as ever.

We were sitting on his wide verandah overlooking the Ping river; his two boxer dogs sprawled at our feet. In the next door room two old Khmer monks were bent over their palm-leaf scrolls. They looked as old as the scrolls they were translating. The late afternoon hush was broken only by low chanting and the chatter of insects. It might well have been a temple compound in the now lost world of

Phnom Penh. As night descended like a curtain on the house, we agreed that, wherever life sent us, the lands of the Mekong would be our spiritual home; the place by which we measured our happiness. And in a changing world, it is the Mekong, the main artery and lifeline of this corner of Southeast Asia, that provides the continuity with our past.

Some rivers are so still, so complacent, so dead that they leave one's heart indifferent. The Mekong is not one of them. To see it in full spate as it thunders over the Koh Khong falls in a welter of foam in the rainy season, is to know its awesome power; I have never been able to stand on its tall banks and look down at its great sweep of moving water without the urge to go round the next bend to explore the wonders that may be in store.

During the war, such exploration was obviously not feasible; nowadays, it can still be hazardous in the extreme. The war is over, and yet it is not *really* over. Cambodia is still dangerously unsettled. There is little sign of a resurrection and it may never be able to wash out the blood from its history. Laos has finally emerged from its years of communist Pathet Lao-induced coma, but mourns its royal family, dead in a re-education camp. There is banditry in the wilder jungles of the country. In Vietnam there is still a schism between the people of the old communist north and the defeated south.

I have travelled hundreds of miles on the Mekong, from the clutter of Phnom Penh to where it crosses the border into Laos. Further north, I have travelled almost the entire length of the majestic stretch flowing from the Chinese border. For miles, the Mekong cuts through steep-sided hills before arriving at the dreamy, unspoilt former royal

279

capital, Luang Prabang. I have journeyed too, on its lower reaches where it flows steadily through Vietnam towards the South China Sea. Here and there, I thought I caught a glimpse of what those early French explorers might have seen one hundred years ago, as they battled their way upriver with extraordinary energy and courage in search of a new river road to southern China.

The Mekong can never again be the savage river it was in the epoch of those tough explorers. Materialism and mass tourism have intruded with their fateful touch; one has to go a long way now to hear parakeets calling to the moon or a panther crying to its mate in the jungle, as Henri Mouhot describes in his diaries. Mouhot wrote: 'If I must die here, where so many other wanderers have left their bones, I shall be ready when my hour comes.'

On 15 October 1861, he set off for Luang Prabang on the banks of the Mekong. A diary entry four days later reads, 'Attacked by fever.' His final entry was written on 29 October. 'Have pity on me, oh my God . . .' it says. Mouhot was buried where he died on the banks of the Nan river, a tributary of the Mekong, a few miles from Luang Prabang. His faithful dog Tin-Tine was later found howling over his grave.

I remember one river journey in Cambodia. The evening shadows were falling and the orange light of the setting sun was turning grey. Soon there would be nothing; sky and river would be blotted out. But in that light the Mekong was everything a tropical river should be. On its banks, at intervals, were traces of village life. Fishing is the breath of life to Indo-China, and fishermen were pulling in their nets as they have done for centuries, at the end of the day's catch.

Their boats, hollowed tree-trunks of canoes, rocked up and down in the waves. Kingfishers darted over the swollen waters.

Nature spoke with nightfall. From a thousand arbours in the forest came the hum of insects. Then darkness dropped. The silence became complete. The moon rose and crept through the clouds, its shifting light forming obscure patterns on the waters. I felt the river carrying my body on a current of happiness. A host of memories passed before my eyes: strolls by moonlight through the temples of Angkor; the warmth and smile of a child's face. Aspects of Cambodia which are true and good. I always hope that the perfect combination of time, place and love that made Indo-China unique, a Paradise for me, will come together again. I am ever hopeful, but how difficult it is to believe that it ever can.